Angelica Malin is founder and editor-in-chief of *About Time Magazine*, the UK's leading lifestyle website. An award-winning entrepreneur, who launched her now six-figure business straight out of university, Angelica helps aspiring entrepreneurs through her platform, events and #SheStartedIt podcast. In January 2021, her first book *#SheMadeIt: A Toolkit for Female Founders in the Digital Age* was published by Kogan Page and reached #4 in Amazon's bestselling career guides. Her second book, *Unattached: Essays on Singlehood*, was published by Square Peg and was a #2 bestseller in feminist criticism.

In 2019, Angelica was shortlisted for BSME's Editors' Editor of the Year and has featured in campaigns for brands such as NatWest, Asto and Courier Media. Angelica is a dynamic event speaker and moderator, who is passionate about creating more spaces to explore starting your business, going freelance or developing a portfolio career. Through her work, Angelica has been featured in *Forbes*, *Real Business*, *Elle*, the *Telegraph* and *Business Insider*.

Passionate about female entrepreneurship, Angelica launched #SheStartedItLIVE in 2019, a festival of female empowerment that brings together female CEOs, thought leaders and aspiring entrepreneurs under one roof. A fresh voice on UK entrepreneurship and self-employment, Angelica regularly features on national radio and TV, most recently on *Good Morning Britain*, TalkRadio, BBC Radio 4 and LBC.

The PR Bootcamp

Take Your Business from Invisible to Unstoppable

Angelica Malin

ROBINSON

ROBINSON

First published in Great Britain in 2022
by Robinson

10 9 8 7 6 5 4 3 2 1

Copyright © Angelica Malin, 2022

A CIP catalogue record for this book
is available from the British Library.

ISBN: 978-1-47214-724-0

Typeset in Sentinel and Scala Sans
by Mousemat Design Limited.

Printed and bound in Great Britain by
Clays Ltd, Elcograf S.p.A.

Papers used by Robinson are from well-
managed forests and other responsible
sources.

MIX
Paper from
responsible sources
FSC® C104740

Robinson
An imprint of
Little, Brown Book Group
Carmelite House
50 Victoria Embankment
London EC4Y 0DZ

An Hachette UK Company
www.hachette.co.uk

www.littlebrown.co.uk

How To Books are published by
Robinson, an imprint of Little,
Brown Book Group. We welcome
proposals from authors who have
first-hand experience of their
subjects. Please set out the aims of
your book, its target market and its
suggested contents in an email to
howto@littlebrown.co.uk.

For Chez and Carla;
may we always bask in the warmth
of a Sunday night sofa session together.

Contents

Introduction

If you've picked up this book, then you're probably wanting more. More from your business. More from your career. More opportunities. More contacts. More flow. PR gives you that – and, you guessed it, more.

PR is the ultimate door-opener; it invites you into a new world, one filled with exciting opportunities, a bigger audience and greater visibility. Getting yourself featured in newspapers, magazines, on podcasts and on TV and radio opens your business up to so much potential; more people will see and engage with your work, and publicity can take your business global.

As you'll see throughout this book, publicity has the ability to totally transform your career. Publicity is transformative and far-reaching – and it begins by simply putting yourself out there. Seeking publicity takes confidence; you have to believe in yourself, your business and your story, and articulate your pitch in a clever way.

And the great news is that you can start right away – with the help of this book, you'll learn the fundamentals of what makes a great PR story and how to pitch it in a compelling way to editors. We'll be looking at the nuances of PR – how it's changed in recent years thanks to the boom in influencer and social media marketing – and what tangible assets you need to sell your story. We'll also be hearing from experts in the PR industry, who will be sharing their top tips, and founder success stories, who have leveraged PR to increase their brand visibility.

This book will share secrets rarely revealed by journalists and editors on how to get featured in their publication – we'll be peeking behind the curtain of some of the UK's most prominent publications and learning how you, too, can get publicity for your business.

ABOUT ME

Why me? While I don't have a traditional PR agency background, much of my career has been focused around storytelling and crafting a creative pitch. For the last ten years, I've been editor-in-chief of About Time Magazine, one of the UK's leading lifestyle sites. I'm also an award-winning entrepreneur and author of *#SheMadeIt: A Toolkit for Female Founders in the Digital Age* and *Unattached: Essays on Singlehood*, which were both bestselling books.

I've worked hard over the years to create my own publicity, and I've been featured in *Forbes, Real Business, Business Insider* and *The Times.* I'm a regular commentator on TV and radio on entrepreneurship, start-ups and women in business, featuring on LBC, Sky News and TalkRadio as a business expert. I also write extensively for different publications in a freelance capacity, including the *Evening Standard, Grazia,* Refinery29 and the *Daily Telegraph.* Working across many publications and platforms, I've developed a strong sense of what different publications are looking for in terms of a good story and how best to position yourself to get coverage.

This isn't a 'traditional' PR book, as we're not following a set of rules here on how to get publicity. Instead we're looking more closely at the relationship between journalists and those wanting publicity, and how you can create genuine, mutually beneficial relationships that will serve your long-term goals. Let's get started!

CHAPTER ONE

Why Every Business
Needs a PR Strategy

Businesses of every size can benefit from having a well-considered, strategic PR plan, one that reflects the brand's overarching goals and desired positioning within the media landscape – and you don't need to spend thousands of pounds to get started with this either.

Whether you're a solopreneur, a thriving direct-to-consumer brand or a global business, there are numerous benefits that PR can provide. In my view, there's no company too big or small for press – all businesses should be thinking about a PR strategy. In fact, fledging start-ups can often attract the most attention, as reading about new business ventures are innovative and inspiring.

Why PR? Well, PR adds credibility to your business. PR has intangible and far-reaching benefits, which you simply can't put a price on. Getting featured in media outlets and setting yourself up as a thought-leader in your industry puts you in a position of strength; you become *the* go-to person for commentary, insight and expertise. This creates a flow and ease with your work, which, as I see it, is unparalleled with anything else you can do to support your business. PR is a superpower for your business and it's something you can do yourself, how great is that?

Many people think PR is simply getting mentioned in the press, but it's so much more than that. It's everything you do to promote and increase visibility of your business. So, first, let's look at what PR is – and what it isn't. The media landscape has changed so much in the last few years, especially with the shift towards digital and remote working during the pandemic, and our definition of PR needs to adapt accordingly. PR is anything and everything that helps get your business talked about, including social media and influencer and brand relations.

WHAT IS PR?

PR – or public relations – in its true definition refers to the strategic communication from an organisation to the public to maintain or cultivate a public image.

PR is what other people say about you. It's how your work and brand are perceived by others, and the efforts you undertake to build a positive brand image.

It's also so much more than that.

PR, as I see it, is about how the public feels and interacts with your company. It's about image, yes, but it's also about connection and appeal. It's what springs to mind when the name of your company is mentioned, how people engage with and respond to the content you post online, how individuals feel when a speaker from your company is on stage. PR is about the emotional connection you're able to build with individuals through your work, which, in turn, leads to sales, opportunities and results.

We all have relationships – with the brands we buy from, the companies whose services we use, the experts we trust – and PR is a fast-track for building these relationships. PR is about getting in front of your audience and creating trust with them. Getting featured in the press is a medium for nurturing relationships with your desired audience. If you've found other effective methods to help you build those relationships, such as Instagram, TikTok or email marketing, then traditional PR can complement this.

Getting featured in the media helps build your credibility, thus strengthening the bond with your audience. Word of mouth is often cited as the most powerful method for getting business traction; with PR, you simply get in front of more mouths.

PR is a crucial part of any marketing strategy, especially one that is digitally focused, as lots of publications are digital-first now. Many business owners shy away from having a PR strategy because they believe (wrongly) that they need a big budget to do so or need to be able to afford an external PR agency. This means that PR often falls to the bottom of a to-do list for when the company feels ready – which may never come.

Let me tell you this: you don't need to feel totally ready to start pitching. And you don't need an agency to do it for you. To date, the best publicity I've received has been of my own making and I truly believe that if you master the skill of handling your own publicity and getting media attention, you give yourself a true skill that you can carry through in any venture or industry.

WHAT MAKES GOOD PR?

Good PR is subjective; it's what works within your personal goals and desired outcome. They say there's no such thing as bad press – although I do think there's such a thing as strategic press, and it's beneficial to consider what 'good' press would look and feel like to you.

Emily Keogh, founder of Palm PR, a travel and hospitality specialist PR agency, offers up a nice definition of what makes good PR, which we can use as a launchpad for thinking about your PR strategy for you.

For Emily, this is what good PR looks like:

The execution and successful application of a PR activation or campaign relies on a thorough understanding of the brand. Whether your PR process is being headed up internally or externally by an agency, it's crucial to get under the skin of the brand, its ethos and its consumer audience.

When implementing an integrated campaign, at Palm we undertake a thorough analysis of the brand's audience base – what they like, where they eat, what they read . . . Knowing this before setting the objective of the campaign allows us to be hyper-targeted.

The success of the campaign is based on knowledge of the landscape and what it is the brand wants to achieve. Whether it's increased sales, brand awareness, reputation management or the promotion of a new product, good PR is the combination of meticulously planned communications, in the brand language, placed in relevant spaces your audience (or soon-to-be customer) will be.

Brands looking to work alongside an agency should consider working with true specialists in their sector as it's crucial for your team to be fully engaged and tuned in to the category to effectively promote the brand and deliver strong results.

WHAT COUNTS AS PR?

Traditionally, PR was centred around newspapers and magazines, but with the boom in social and digital media over the last few years, our understanding of PR needs to shift accordingly.

A few years ago, PR would be defined by getting featured in the press – this might be magazines, newspapers or TV. Fast-forward to today, social media plays a valuable role in a PR plan, as this is another way you'll be talking to your consumer. By way of further explanation, here are the different forms of media you may want to consider for your PR plan:

NEWSPAPERS

Traditional print press is great for building credibility. It's arguably the hardest place to land coverage, because it requires you to have good contacts, to create newsworthy stories and work to tight deadlines, but print coverage is powerful for brand-building. There are lots of digital-first newspapers too – anything that has a strong focus on the news cycle would come under this umbrella. While journalists write for both online and print, trying to cultivate relationships with print-focused writers is a good starting point if you're wanting to land coverage in traditional print media.

MAGAZINES

Magazines, both print and online, are great for profiling opportunities, product placements and 'real life' stories. If you've got a compelling story to tell, magazines are the place to go. There are loads of great ones out there, and where you choose to focus your attention will depend on your industry and niche – everything from women's glossy magazines and lifestyle titles to specialist food and well-being magazines. Print seems to be a dying art, as many magazines are now digital-only, such as *Marie Claire*, *Red* and *Time Out*.

BROADCAST

Broadcast media is a fantastic place to be if you're a business founder and want to position yourself as an expert in your field. Broadcast media includes all visual and audio-led platforms, such as TV and radio. Pitching for broadcast media has a different set of rules, in my experience, and we'll be focusing later in the book on how to prime yourself for broadcast opportunities, as producers in this space work in a different way to the traditional print press.

PODCASTS

The podcast boom is real. It's estimated that there will be around twenty million podcast listeners in the UK by 2024 and the number of new shows in the podcast space is growing by the day. Podcasts are a fantastic medium for getting your voice heard and bringing new fans to your work. If you want a rich and diverse PR plan, you want to land yourself on some popular podcasts too. You may also want to consider starting your own podcast as another way to amplify your brand. If so, below are some tips from leading podcast host Francesca Specter on how to do so.

FIVE GOLDEN RULES FOR CREATING YOUR OWN PODCAST

Francesca Specter is creator and host of the Alonement podcast. Here she shares her top tips for creating a sucessful podcast:

Define your niche

Your podcast niche will likely be something at least loosely related to your business – however, it's very important to be able to define exactly what this is. A vague one-word subject isn't enough – nor is a messy list of things you'd like to discuss: you will need a clear, bold sentence that summarises what your show is about, and what you're asking your guests. Say you've a jewellery business, and you want to create a related podcast which explores the concept of 'gifting'. You'll want a sentence that sounds something like, 'Give and Receive: This is a podcast where we ask guests about the lasting significance of gifts, where we ask them about the most important gift they have ever given, and the one they've received – and why they mattered.'

Identify your listener

It's absolutely integral to think about your listener. You might think you already know your client or customer from a marketing perspective (and of course there's going to be plenty of overlap here), but there are some important questions you'll want to consider that are specific to podcast consumption.

- When are they listening? (On their commute? In their leisure time?)
- *Why* are they listening? (Do they want to be inspired? Or educated? Or simply entertained?)

- Where are they listening? (In the car with kids? On a solitary walk? In the bath?)

All these answers will go on to inform the packaging of your podcast, from the artwork to the episode length.

Prioritise sound quality

No one's expecting studio-level perfection, but you do need to make sure your audio quality is high. This means no distracting background noise, consistent volume levels, and a rich vocal quality (i.e. not a far away, echoey sound). Prevention is better than cure here – if your recording set-up is good then you can easily avoid problems down the line. You'll need a decent mid-range mic set-up (I use the Rode PodMic, a dynamic mic, which is a good choice because it picks up only close-range sound rather than background noise, connected to my laptop via a Zoom recorder) and a quiet, well-insulated room. If you are new to audio, there are plenty of resources for this online, including a coaching service I offer for beginner DIY podcasters available at podcasttoplatform.com. However, you might also find it more efficient to ask for help from a freelance producer early on, together with getting honest listening experience feedback from friends for your first couple of episodes.

Pick the right name

There's no golden rule of how to do this, but picking the right name is a smart thing to get right the first time – and stick with it. While all the other elements of your show are easily changed (including the cover art, jingle and even the whole format of the show), the name is the strand that ties everything together. If you can name it after your existing brand, that will reap rewards for everything from memorability to Search Engine

Optimisation (SEO). Alternatively, just try to take it back to the 'why' of your podcast – think about what your ideal listener would want, and choose a name based on those factors.

Focus on having a good conversation

It may sound simple, but the mark of a good podcast in a nutshell is that it's a conversation your listeners would like to be part of. So, focus on creating that for your listener. If it's meant to entertain, then make it entertaining – don't be afraid to have fun if that's what you want the person listening to share in. If it's meant to be informative, keep coming back to the value that your conversation gives. This isn't the time for obsessing over interview technique (or imposing too many rules on your host, if you've hired one that isn't yourself). Podcast is, by its nature, more informal than a broadcast interview – and your listeners will know that. It's simply about having a good chat.

Alonement podcast
https://www.alonement.com/

INFLUENCERS + BLOGS

Moving away from 'traditional' media, arguably the biggest explosion in the last few years has been influencer marketing. Nowadays, you wouldn't create a marketing plan without having an influencer strategy too, and there are whole agencies dedicated to building and brokering relationships between brands and influencers.

Working with influencers can be an incredibly powerful tool for getting attention for your brand. The results can be tracked quite clearly in terms of return on investment, which is the beauty of online media. But with such a saturated space, getting your partnerships right and working with the right influencers for your brand is key. This is something we will explore in a later chapter, especially how to work out who is the right fit for you and how to approach influencers.

Blogs are another tool that can be useful in a PR strategy. While blogging may feel a little dated now, there are still lots of blogs that have great SEO and readership, and that fit a particular niche for your demographic. It's great to think outside the box with PR; there might be outlets that are a lot smaller in terms of readership and MUUs (monthly unique users), but have a very specific community that can benefit you.

SOCIAL MEDIA

Beyond working with influencers, being strategic with your own social media is crucial to any PR plan. While we define PR as what other people say about you, thinking about what you say about yourself and your own company matters – the look, sound and feel of your business will help you stand out from the rest and build your unique business blueprint.

Coming up with a strong social media strategy that includes Instagram, TikTok, LinkedIn and Twitter can be so valuable within a larger PR plan, as it means you are making the most of the channels available to you. This helps build appeal with the press, setting yourself up for more opportunities and creating buzz. Thus I'll be focusing attention in the book on how you can get your social media on-point and create value in your business.

EVENTS + SPEAKING

Events are another valuable part of a PR plan to consider. Whether it's your company's CEO delivering a keynote, being part of a panel talk or hosting webinars, not only are speaking events press-worthy in themselves, but they will also help you build a 'face' to your brand, making it more personable. Looking for speaking opportunities is easier than you think and securing high-profile speaking slots is again great for credibility.

These elements can all work together to help you build a well-rounded, multi-media PR strategy, one that works towards your specific goals and desired outcomes. Of course, you can't do everything at once, so consider what's most important to your business right now and where you might focus your energy – it's easier and more efficient to pursue one or two key platforms mentioned above than try to do everything at once.

CASE STUDY:
ALEXANDER HICKSON ON DIGITAL-FIRST PR

Alexander Hickson is a digital PR lead, who helps brands amplify their reach through digital content. Here, he shares his insights on what makes a winning digital-first PR campaign:

Name: Alexander Hickson
Age: 25
Job Title: Digital PR lead

What is a digital-first PR strategy?

Digital-first is about understanding and activating the digital benefits of your campaigns and PR efforts. For many years, the goal of PR has been to gain 'earned media', and have brands and companies talked about by the press and public alike. A digital-first strategy looks at effective ways to measure these efforts, through website traffic, conversions and SEO benefits. The more data gained through these methods, the more tailored and effective your PR campaigns can become. Understanding the audience that engages with your brand's content allows you to build targeted campaigns, and tailor your outreach to publications and press you know the key audience will seek out.

Why is it important for businesses to focus on their digital strategy?

Ultimately, we want to be working smarter. Having a strong and robust digital strategy that lays the foundations for your PR and social media campaigns means that they can be measurable and adaptable. As the relationship between agency and client grows, a good digital strategy is something that is honed and refined regularly to make sure existing and emerging client goals can be met.

What are the building blocks of a great digital-first campaign?

- Relevancy: Is this a topic people are discussing now, or will be in the near future?
- Audience: Who are you looking to target?
- Emotion: You need to know what emotion you want to evoke from your end audience, is it shock, nostalgia, happiness?
- Strong data: Not all campaigns rely on data, but having this to bolster your campaigns and creativity provides multiple angles.
- Innovative multi-channel execution: Why is this digital-first? Consider whether you want to drive links to a website, or have this engaged with on social media – it has to feel and be different so that it can't just be mentioned in a column in a newspaper.

What's the most successful digital campaign you've ever done for a client and why do you think it worked?

The most successful in terms of SEO impact and revenue was actually for my own brand, launching my candle company Flaming Crap. In many ways, it was a test of the power of using digital PR as the sole marketing tool to launch a completely new ecommerce brand. It gathered 300+ links and generated over £15,000 in revenue from an idea, a simple photoshoot and a press release.

We created a candle that was multi-scented like the year 2020 including hand sanitiser, banana bread and scents of 'Joe Exotic' to reminisce around the first lockdown. We launched this campaign the week prior to the US election in which Donald Trump lost, and found it exploded across all media in the UK, US and internationally. It played into a light-hearted, topical comment on the year, that offered the 'perfect tonic' to the US election coverage. As well as driving hundreds of links to our website and product page, helping with keyword rankings, it drove thousands of new users to our site during November and December 2020, which led to hundreds of conversions and increased revenue.

What's the most common thing brands overlook when it comes to digital-first PR?

Brands often stump themselves by thinking some of their existing media or PR activity can't be leveraged towards their digital goals. Often existing content or previous campaigns that sit on a site are the first place I would look to see if there are any quick wins to amplify a digital-first campaign. However, one of the main things is understanding what those goals are.

Does the brand want links to help with SEO goals? Do they want links to drive traffic? Do they want to increase engagement on their social media channels? Or do they want all of the above?

Often those goals will define the execution of that campaign, not necessarily the idea – a good idea can be utilised across multiple media channels.

Any advice on how to execute a successful digital campaign using social media?

Social media can be harnessed in multiple ways for a successful digital campaign:

- Inspiration: researching trends or conversations, memes or ways people are engaging with certain content.
- Strategy: you can look at engagement of topics to see what's producing results, this is essential in making sure your campaign aligns with your digital goals.
- Execution: often some of my most successful pitches occurred through building relationships or sending pitches through social media. Not in the same way I would via email,

but by helping understand the landscape of the niche I was pitching to.

What do you think the future of digital PR is?
Soon I think 'digital PR' and 'traditional PR' will become one. We're already seeing 'traditional' techniques used for digital goals. Anyone who thinks digital PR is just beneficial for SEO is only scratching the surface.

The success of digital PR can be measured in ways that other PR methods can't be. However, I do think we'll see Google focusing on relevancy and sentiment more when analysing a website's backlink profile.

Follow Alexander on Twitter
https://twitter.com/alexhicksonpr

WHY DOES PR MATTER?

PR matters because we all want to have successful, thriving businesses, but there's a ceiling on how much you can do for your business yourself and publicity helps take your career to the next level. Whether it's reaching more customers, going viral on TikTok and getting an influx of sales, or being endorsed by a credible publication, the benefits of PR can convert into so many factors for your business.

PR is important because we demand more from brands every day: we now expect businesses to act like people, to have ethics, values and an ethos, to have a social conscience and to be doing good in the world. We expect more from brands in the way that they act and treat the world around them – the planet, their customers, other businesses – and PR is one of the ways that you communicate the good that you're doing in the world. It provides a peek behind the curtain of your business and tells a story that might not otherwise be shared. That story matters.

To me, the fundamental principle of PR is: have a good story and pitch it in a compelling way. Sounds simple right? Well, it is, if you *know* what makes a good story and a captivating pitch, which is what I'm going to reveal in this book, alongside other secrets.

WHAT ARE THE BENEFITS OF PR?

There are loads of fantastic benefits of PR, and if you've bought this book, I'm sure you don't need a lot of convincing that it's beneficial for your business. Let's highlight some of the key advantages of receiving attention in the press and what you should be thinking about when building your PR plan. Here are some ways it can strategically benefit your brand:

CREDIBILITY

This one is particularly relevant if you're a business with a prominent founder or CEO. A credible business is one that is trustworthy, reliable and has great customer relationships, one that is believed in and supported by its audience. If you're featured in a credible publication, such as the *Sunday Times* or *Business Insider*, your credibility automatically grows as your brand is aligned with and elevated by theirs.

BRAND-BUILDING

You might have the best brand in the world but has anybody heard about it? And if they haven't, how are you going to spread the word? Being featured in a digital publication such as *Metro*, which has hundreds of thousands of daily readers, will give your business the super-charge it needs. PR is one of the quickest and most effective ways to build noise around your brand if you have the fundamentals of a good business in place to start with.

LEADERSHIP

If you want to be a leader in your industry, PR can be the difference that sets you apart. The leaders and experts that are featured in the press take up more space than others, and you can start to lead in your industry simply by virtue of being the press's go-to person on a topic. That's why 'thought-leadership' content does so well in the press; being press-worthy is also about being willing and able to lead others.

PARTNERSHIPS

Another key benefit of PR is it can facilitate more partnership opportunities. By widening yourself up to a bigger audience, you'll find more opportunities come your way and other companies will get in touch wanting to work together. Nothing succeeds like success itself. Partnerships might look like splitting profits with a charity, co-hosting an event series with a publication, or doing social media takeovers with an influencer. The more touchpoints you can create with your business and potential new customers, clients or fans, the better.

FUTURE-PROOFING

In many ways, I think PR can future-proof your business. If we take the pandemic as an example, so many businesses were forced to pivot into new areas or totally change their business model. The businesses that already had strong relationships with their audience can pivot more effectively and take their customers along on the journey with them, because there's a foundation of trust and connection. And it doesn't hurt that when they do pivot, there are already relationships in place with the press to spread the word.

CASE STUDY:
NATALIE TRICE ON HOW TO CREATE A PR STRATEGY

Natalie Trice is an author, career coach and PR consultant who has worked in the media for twenty-five years. She's also the bestselling author of *PR School: Your Time to Shine*. Here, Natalie shares her top tips for how to create a PR strategy that works for you:

Name: Natalie Trice
Age: 47
Job title: PR coach

When thinking about building a PR plan, where should you start?

Many people are scared of PR because they don't quite know what it is, what is involved, and what the outcomes are. That is fine, but changing those elements is key to starting. This book, talking to people and research can all help you get to grips with PR, and the more you can learn and understand, the better.

In addition to this, just think about your ideal client and the media they consume because they are who needs to see you, so you need to be where they are.

What makes a great story in your eyes?

Consider the target audience, what they want to read, listen to and find out more about. Journalists, like all of us, are busy. What will make them stop and think? Why should they care about what you're telling them? What makes this story interesting for them? Always relate your story back to the target audience – consider what they want to read, listen to and find out more about.

You might think that a new member of staff joining you is big news, but an editor at *The Times* might not. Nevertheless, you could comment on a wider piece on market recovery for small businesses in the wake of Covid.

What advice do you give your clients for creating stand-out stories?

Read the press. Look at the publications you think your clients read (you can ask them if you don't know) and see what stories they use, the kind of interviews they print and the topics they write about. The more you can do to become knowledgeable, the more likely it is you will start to see your own stories.

How can businesses help themselves get press?

If you want to be seen in the press you need to be ready with content, images, an online presence, and if you say you are going to work with a journalist, don't let them down at the last minute.

Where do you look for press opportunities?

As a seasoned PR consultant, I am always on the lookout for opportunities for me and my clients, but I would say that Twitter is a great place. As well as many journalists being on the platform, there is the #journorequest hashtag which is used when the press are looking for help with a whole multitude of stories.

What one thing do you wish more people knew about pitching to the press?

PR isn't free! No, you aren't paying cold hard cash for ad space, but it's an investment in time, images, creativity and energy – none of which are free!

Natalie Trice
https://natalietrice.co.uk/

WORKBOOK: HOW PR CAN BENEFIT MY BUSINESS

At the end of every chapter, there are some questions to consider about what you've learnt and how you can apply this learning to your business. Use these sections within the book to start building your own PR plan. Grab a pen and paper and answer the questions below:

1. What will the main areas of focus for your PR plan be? List the three areas.

2. Why are these areas of focus the most relevant for your business?

3. What three things do you want to achieve with your PR plan?

4. What words spring to mind when you think about how you want to be perceived in the press?

5. What benefits to your business would you like to see with your PR plan?

CHAPTER TWO

How to Build an Objectives-driven PR Plan

In this chapter, we'll be looking at how to build an objectives-driven, strategic PR plan, one that has clear goals and outcomes in mind. In my experience, founders are often overwhelmed by the question of where to start with PR, so they think that getting *any* PR is better than no PR, which is not necessarily wrong, but it can lead to inconsistent results. In the following chapter, we'll be setting out some clear objectives for your PR campaign, which you can track and use to measure the success of your outreach.

Remember: random actions get random results. Daily, consistent habits will help you towards your PR goals – and there's lots you can do to support your efforts yourself, without an agency. Even if you're just starting up, you can still be intentional about your approach to PR. You're never too small as a business to have a strategy.

The kind of press you're hoping to secure will depend on your unique business goals and objectives, so it's a good idea to start there and work backwards. Let's first explore what you're trying to achieve with PR and create a blueprint for achieving results based on those goals.

So, let me ask you this: what do you want? I mean what do you really, really want? Beyond just publicity, what do you want for your business and career? PR is one of the stepping stones towards the most exciting, dynamic version of your career – but you have to get clear on your vision first.

Is it recognition for the work you do?

Is it more speaking opportunities?

Is it more sales?

Is it brand awareness?

Make sure the answers are compelling and personal to you.

Below is an exercise that will help you identify what the unique goals are for you and your business.

EXERCISE: **IDENTIFYING YOUR PR GOALS**

Grab a pen and paper and answer the questions below in as much detail as possible:

1. **What do you personally want to be known for?**

2. **Why does this matter to you?**

3. **How do you think getting press is going to support your overall business goals?**

4. **Which networks and places do you want your business to be known in? How would you like it to be received in the press?**

5. **What are your dream publications to be featured in?**

6. **What publications do you think are most aligned with your brand?**

7. **If you were to pick three key words for how you want to be seen in the press, what would they be?**

8. **Are there any similar businesses that successfully garnered press attention that can inspire you?**

9. **Are there any business owners you'd like to model yourself on?**

Top tip: You need to have a strong reason for wanting press, because PR is not something that will happen overnight. If you

> *have a powerful reason that you can come back to, it will help you stick at the daily actions needed to move your PR plan along. So, find something that feels compelling to you.*

Based on the answers to the above, you should have a sense of what you're trying to achieve with press – paying particular attention to how you want to be perceived in the press will help with the kind of language you use to describe your business. Additionally, having a list of dream publications for coverage is good to work towards. Often, when I work one-to-one with someone, they don't just want press for press's sake; they have been slogging away for years on their business, product or service, and they just want things to be easier, for there to be more flow and ease with work.

Media attention can help facilitate that flow, because the higher your profile, the more naturally clients and opportunities come your way – without feeling the need for constant hustle. The greater your public profile and visibility, honestly, the easier work becomes. And we all want an easy life, right?

Once you've answered these questions, you can start thinking about the kind of outlets you should approach. For example, if you answered that you wanted to be known as an expert or thought-leader in your industry, you might want to go after specialist titles that are influential in your industry. If you wanted to generate more sales through press, then your best bet is going to be glossy titles and women's magazines that have a large online readership. If you've got a particular topic you feel passionate about, perhaps getting onto podcasts can be incorporated into your PR strategy.

Figuring out the right outlets for your business is a great starting point, as it can be overwhelming and unproductive to adopt the blanket approach of wanting to be everywhere and seen by everyone – this leads to extensive PR mailers that rarely get much pick-up. It is much better to have three or four key titles that you'd really like to feature in, and create well-researched individual pitches based on those targeted publications. If you're not sure what the right publications for your PR plan are, answer the questions about your ideal reader below.

EXERCISE: **IDEAL READER FOR YOUR BUSINESS**

Consider the demographic of an ideal reader that you'd like to discover you. This work goes beyond your average 'ideal client' template, as you need to be thinking about what your ideal client might be reading and spending time on online. This will help you create a more considered strategy, as you'll be talking to the right person for your business, one who is likely to go from follower to fan.

Take a moment to consider these questions:

AGE – What age bracket is your ideal reader? Online publications tend to have a younger readership than print titles.

READERSHIP – Are they likely to be a print or online reader? How do they like to consume their news and information? Are they active on social media?

INTERESTS – What is someone who reads this publication interested in? Pick two or three key interests that would resonate with your ideal reader and then look for publications that create content around these topics, such as well-being, finance or business.

LOCATION – Where are they based? Local papers and magazines are often overlooked, but if you run a locally focused business, they can be so great for word of mouth in your locale.

INCOME – How much do they earn? What do they spend their money on? Thinking about the income bracket and spending habits of your ideal customer will help you discover the kind of things they might be reading – high-end magazines like *Spear's* or the *Financial Times* will appeal to a higher financial bracket than magazines such as *Grazia*.

CASE STUDY:
AMANDA FITZGERALD ON HOW TO IDENTIFY
YOUR TARGET PUBLICATIONS

Amanda FitzGerald is a PR and visibility strategist, also known as The Ultimate Door Opener. She is passionate about training entrepreneurs to successfully pitch to the press and get super visible using the power of PR so that they have a surge of new client enquiries and a major confidence booster all at the same time. Here she shares her top tips for landing your dream publications:

Name: Amanda FitzGerald
Age: 51
Job title: The Ultimate Door Opener

When a business owner comes to you wanting press, where do you start?

When a business owner comes to me wanting press, I like to tell them that doing your own PR is possible. After all, I managed to get featured in most of the dailies and glossy magazines when I had two very small toddlers and a product that no one really understood. I share a bit of my backstory and, in doing so, they take inspiration and often have some 'aha' moments along the way.

My PR journey first started back in 2008 when I was running my luxury knitwear brand. It was a fledgling company set up just after the birth of my first child. I created a company that imported alpaca knitwear from Peru as we had been given so many lovely brightly coloured ponchos, *chullos* (typical Peruvian-style woollen hats) and accessories from our relatives in Peru. These were widely admired by parents at the baby groups I was part of, and I kept getting stopped in the street by passers-by who would admire the colourful and different garments.

This gave me the brainwave to replicate my mother's business which imported beads from around the world. My mother's company was a hugely successful mail order company in the '80s and '90s and the business grew from a database of 400 names to over 40,000 all thanks to the PR efforts she first put in. Later on she appointed a PR agent as my mother recognised the power of PR in reaching new audiences.

When I set up my children's knitwear brand, I soon expanded the offering to adults as well as to homewares, but all the while I was competing with the very well-established companies out there – Peruvian Connection, Brora, Pure Collection, Spirit of the Andes, etc. I was also competing with a well-known and hugely popular wool – cashmere – and no one had really heard of alpaca back then.

Despite all these potential barriers, I was not put off. I decided that I would try to get media coverage as I certainly couldn't afford the big ads that the competitors were taking out or the kinds of fees they were paying their expensive PR agencies.

So it was a case of David and Goliath!

The first phase that should not be overlooked is research and my first PR 'aha' moment was to consider *who* my customers were and to work out which publications and news outlets they consumed.

The second very important action was to get some clippings of my competitors' placements – be it adverts or publicity – and to take note of those media outlets.

I then got a good idea of where I should start to make my approaches. There is no point spending huge efforts pitching to a so-called 'dream outlet' if your target audience doesn't even read it.

The next bit of research was to get the contact details of the journalists for the sections in the glossy magazines or newspapers. This was back in 2008, so I would go to WHSmith to purchase the publications.

This is vital as I hear so often from journalists and editors that a pet peeve is to be pitched to when it is abundantly clear that the person has not even read the magazine.

I would read the magazines and get to know who wrote the pieces and familiarise myself with their writing style. I would learn who the editors for the shopping pages were, as well as going straight to the masthead of the magazine (this is where the contact details are housed) and I would create a hit list of names, emails and telephone numbers.

I call this research phase the 'tune in' phase as you're tuning in to the news coverage so that you can react in case a story crops up that may be relevant for you to create a pitch around, as well as doing the very important pre-pitch prep work.

What really helps a business or entrepreneur get media coverage?

While you're doing this background work and finding potential opportunities, it is advisable to do some pre-pitch mindset work as you are likely to be rejected (or rather ignored) more than you are invited to comment or share your high-res images and website links to the product page.

Create a vision board of where you'd like to be featured and create a game plan of how to keep your spirits up when you are in PR campaign mode. You may not hear from the people you've pitched to for a few days or weeks, if ever; you could make a few phone calls and not get anywhere, so treat your pitching to the press as an essential everyday activity that takes you no more than thirty minutes. If you get knocked back, you just need to think about your 'Big Why': why are you running your business?

Your Big Why will keep you going and your vision board will keep you on track, because if you put in the effort, you will be rewarded. So, for your PR toolkit, add: persistence, politeness, patience and courage and this will help you to manage your expectations.

What really works when trying to network and build rapport with journalists?

My strongest recommendation is to be helpful to journalists. If you put yourself in their shoes and realise that they receive up to a thousand pitch emails a week and they need to write up to eight articles a week, you'll see that they are very busy people . . . yet they do need you! They are constantly on the lookout for new case studies, experts, feature ideas and products to share with their audiences, so follow them on Twitter and keep an eye on their feed. Be sure to retweet, like and sometimes share a connection that they may be interested in, so that when your time comes to pitch to them, you're not coming out of the blue; you're already loosely on their radar so it won't be a cold pitch from someone totally random.

Is there a 'secret' to PR?

PR has been called a 'black art' and many people actually fear doing their own PR; however, we can all do our own PR so long as what you pitch is relevant and timely as well as very short and succinct. Don't forget the pressure journalists are under to turn around copy, so be helpful not a hindrance and you will strike up some good relationships.

When you have got your coverage, always thank the journalist. This will deepen your relationship with them as not many people think to say thank you, so you'll be standing out from the crowd!

How can you tell whether something is a strong story to pitch?

You can tell if something is a strong story when it's something new and hasn't been talked about before – like a best kept secret. I have a client, Wendy Andrew, who has had reams of press coverage, she is a pet bereavement counsellor. She writes strong pitches that get picked up as she is a rarity! So try to find out something about your backstory that is a 'golden nugget' which will make you stand out from all the others who are pitching the same journalist.

Amanda Fitzgerald
www.amandapr.com

PITCHING YOUR DREAM PUBLICATIONS

I want to do as much work for you as possible in this book, so below I've highlighted some publications that you might like to include in your strategy across different verticals. The best way to get familiar with these publications is by reading them regularly and taking a keen interest in their content – sign up to their newsletters, follow them on social media, go to their events. If you want to be *in* the media, first you must start by taking an *interest* in the media.

I've also included some top tips for pitching these different publications, many of which I've written for myself or have been featured in, so I have a good sense of what they are looking for. I've also included organisations that have an editorial output as these can also be a great way of building your personal credibility. You can set yourself up as a blogger on these sites and start producing content that will benefit your PR efforts.

This list is by no means exhaustive, and there are lots of publications I haven't included here, especially newer and relatively small ones, but it's a good starting point for some publications to consider within your PR plan.

Note: The media landscape is forever changing, with lots of publications closing or becoming digital-only, so keep a keen eye for any changes. Always pitch the publications that are most active at the time. Most print papers also have an online site, so I've included them once to save duplication, but you may need to find different contacts for each version.

NEWS – PRINT PUBLICATIONS

Newspapers are looking for news. Let me say that again: newspapers are looking for news. Very often, I've worked with individuals who want to be featured in the news but their story is not news itself – or at least it's not newsworthy. It needs to be recent, a 'breaking story' or something with real relevance to the world right now. If you're trying to get featured in a national, you must have a very strong 'hook' or 'sell'. It's really the only rule you need to keep in mind for news pitching: make sure it's news.

Speed is also worth mentioning here. News happens at lightning speed, and your pitching needs to match that. Make sure the story you're pitching is timely and relevant, but get it out there quickly. The lead times will be half of that of digital magazines and lifestyle titles, we're talking about a few hours' turnaround on stories, rather than days or weeks. Make sure you have everything ready to go before pitching an idea – high-res imagery, press release, case studies – whatever you need to sell your story, ensure it's all together before you hit 'send'. Strong imagery is an important asset when selling a news story, make sure you have both portrait and landscape photos in high enough resolution for print.

Guardian
The Times
Daily Telegraph
Financial Times
Daily Mail
Evening Standard
Metro
Sun
Daily Mirror

NEWS – DIGITAL PUBLICATIONS

Independent
Yahoo
Daily Star

Mail Online
Yahoo
Buzzfeed
Huffpost UK
Newsweek
Daily Express

NEWS – BROADCAST MEDIA

Pitching broadcast media is a unique skill and I'll be dedicating a chapter later in the book on how to get broadcast opportunities, but I'll mention here that Twitter is your go-to place for this. Again, speed is crucial in broadcast news, so keep an eye on what's going on in the news and if you have something relevant to move the story along or add insights from your personal experience. Make sure you're following lots of broadcast producers on Twitter so you can spot these opportunities as they arise.

BBC News
Sky News
ITV News
Channel 5 News
CNN International
Reuters

TOP TIPS:
FIVE WAYS TO LAND BROADCAST COVERAGE

Gemma Harris is a publicity expert, with more than twenty years' experience in media relations. She generates A-list coverage for hundreds of self-employed professionals, experts, public-listed companies, corporations and SMEs. Here are her top tips for securing broadcast media coverage:

1. **You've got to be part of the news agenda.** Do you know how to piggyback it to get on air? Are you doing your research? Find out what is coming up over the next year –

awareness days, sales figures, events, VAT, tax, retail sales, quarterly GDP figures, employment figures. Use the Google Trends tool to look at what is coming up for the next year and plan your stories ahead.

2. **Make sure you really know ALL the opportunities you can comment on.** Stay well informed in all the most newsworthy areas of expertise, such as finance, technology, mental health, travel, entrepreneurship, human interest stories and charities with case studies.

3. **Make sure your media list has direct phone numbers** to all the newsdesks, planning desks, diary desks, bureau desks and producers so that it's ready for you to go to as soon as a story breaks.

4. **React quickly and forget the press release.** A short pitch with a rough angle on the back of a breaking story is the way forward. Your email should start: 'Hello X, I am writing to you regarding a breaking story on Y. I represent a client who (include their expertise). If you'd like to have them on air, please call me on . . .'

5. **There are nuances in broadcast PR. Know the right people and how to approach them.** Decide if broadcast PR is right for you: are you prepared? Do you or your spokesperson have at least five years' experience in your field? Once you're in, make sure your client stands out visually and is briefed. If they do a great job first time, the chances are they will be booked again and again.

Follow Gemma on LinkedIn
https://www.linkedin.com/in/gemmaharrislineup

BUSINESS PUBLICATIONS

Business publications want tangible evidence of your success. I've written extensively for *Business Insider* and *Startups* magazine, and the first thing they always ask is: what backs this story up? You need evidence, whether that's stats, data, numbers, turnover or growth numbers to really legitimise and sell your story.

We'll be looking in the next chapter at what makes a good story, but for now, let me say: making money is not a story in and of itself. You need to go beyond the income narrative to tell a captivating business story. This might be trends, predictions, forecasts for an industry, an interesting take on success or an interview that shows a previously undisclosed side of a business. Good business stories are anything but dull; they should be compelling, human and personal.

Forbes
Business Insider
Real Business
Startups.co.uk
Entrepreneur magazine Inc.
Elite Business
Startups magazine
Management Today
SmallBusiness.co.uk
Real Business
Business Matters
City A.M.
CrunchBase

FINANCE TITLES

The same advice goes for finance magazines. While on the surface they appear to be about money, it's not really about the money. Many money magazines also focus on what money means to us, why money matters, how to do more with your money – again, the human and in some ways emotional side of money, and our connection to it. Draw out those aspects in your pitch and you're more likely to land a story.

The Economist
Money Week
Investors' Chronicle
This is Money
Money Saving Expert
Yahoo Finance
Economic Times
Financial Times

WOMEN'S INTEREST MAGAZINES

There are loads of great popular interest magazines, which include features, opinion pieces, trend predictions and product round-ups. Remember to avoid pitching things that have already been covered – this is why it's important to read the magazines regularly. Many of these publications will have both a print and online version, and, although teams often double up, many have separate in-house staff for each version, so make sure you have a clear idea of where you'd like the feature to appear before pitching.

With women's titles, you should be thinking: why does this topic matter to women? How does it affect them? How am I helping or supporting women with my product, service or story? Why would it appeal to them? If you can't find a strong reason why this particular story would resonate with their demographic, it may be better suited elsewhere.

Marie Claire
Stylist
British *Vogue*
Tatler
Cosmopolitan
Hello!
ELLE

Refinery29
OK!
Good Housekeeping
House & Garden
Woman & Home
Prima
The Lady

MEN'S INTEREST MAGAZINES

GQ
Men's Health
Men's Fitness
Esquire

WELL-BEING

The well-being boom is real, and, especially after the pandemic, there's more focus than ever before on well-being, fitness and mental health. Magazines like *Women's Health*, *Runner's World* and *Yoga Magazine* focus more on physical health, whereas magazines such as *Happiful* and *Psychologies* are go-to places for features and insights on mental health. Well-being is a hot topic and if you're operating in this niche, it can be a great area of the press to focus your efforts on.

Women's Health
Psychologies
Happiful
WellBeing
Liz Earle Wellbeing
Hip & Healthy
Thrive Global
Runner's World
Yoga Magazine
Healthy

FASHION PUBLICATIONS

Product placement is its own specialist PR topic and you'd be well advised to get an agency to support you in the early days if you're looking for this kind of coverage, as product placement is very competitive. The key things to remember are to have high-res cut-out imagery, a 'fact sheet' on hand with all the key product info and to be mindful of special days such as Valentine's Day or Father's Day where there may be good opportunities for landing placement in round-ups.

Glamour
Allure
InStyle
Dazed
i-D
Sheerluxe
Grazia
Red
NYLON

TRAVEL PUBLICATIONS

Most travel magazines are now online-only. When trying to land travel stories, there are two main things to consider. One is trends: how are people travelling and why? How does your story fit with those changing travel habits? And the second thing to think about is experience: are you able to offer a journalist an experience of what you're wishing to be covered? The same goes for food and restaurants. You're much more likely to land coverage if they can experience the thing first-hand and write about it from a personal perspective, so put aside some budget if you can host journalists and press for your travel story.

Condé Nast Traveller
Travel + Leisure
Wanderlust
National Geographic

Travel Weekly
Elite Traveler

LIFESTYLE MAGAZINES

Lifestyle magazines, such as *Time Out* and *The Nudge*, cover what's on, entertainment, food, style and more. This is a great place to pitch if you've got an event (in person or virtual) that you'd like covered, or something newsy in the lifestyle space, such as a new restaurant opening. Keep in mind that lots of lifestyle titles like to feature events and venues on their Instagram, so have some 'Gram-worthy pictures at the ready.

TimeOut
About Time Magazine
LondONtheinside
Visit London
The Nudge
Londonist
The Handbook
Secret London
MyLondon
The Resident

LUXURY MAGAZINES

Luxury magazines have a high-end look and feel, so your imagery needs to be suitably luxe. If you're going to invest in anything, it should be quality imagery and video content that can support your story.

How to Spend It
Spear's
Vanity Fair
Billionaire
Harper's Bazaar
Luxury Lifestyle Magazine
The Luxury Editor

COMMENT SECTIONS

Pitching comment pieces can be fun and a great way to spark dialogue. Remember that sometimes getting PR is about stepping out of your comfort zone and getting creative. If you feel strongly about something or are personally affected by something in the news, then why not pitch a comment piece? PR is about being reactive and responding to what's going on in the news cycle. Think about speed for this one too; you don't want to pitch something when the story has already become old news.

The Cut
The Atlantic
The Independent Voices
Guardian
Metro Opinion
Daily Telegraph
iNews
Gal-Dem

FOOD AND DRINK PUBLICATIONS

Think of trends when you're pitching food and drink magazines. Is everyone doing Dry January? Do you have stats to show more people are turning vegan? Have CBD cocktails become the latest thing? Do some research into the most exciting things happening in the food and drink industry right now and use that as your sell. Also partnering with a celebrity chef or foodie influencer can be a great way to get your brand noticed and attract press attention.

BBC Good Food
Food & Wine
The Drinks Business
Bake
Saveur
Olive
Feel Good Food

Imbibe
Bon Appétit
Delicious
Epicurious

TV OPPORTUNITIES

TV producers are fairly reactive, so you really want to be keeping an eye on what's going on in the news. I would be using Twitter strategically to follow producers for both TV and radio here – and keep putting yourself forward for opportunities, even if you don't always hear back. Find contacts on LinkedIn and connect with relevant people in the broadcast space, highlighting your expertise and specialism.

Loose Women – ITV
Jeremy Vine – Channel 5
Steph's Packed Lunch – Channel 4
Morning Live – BBC One
This Morning – ITV
Good Morning Britain – ITV
Lorraine – ITV
GB News

RADIO OPPORTUNITIES

Woman's Hour – BBC Radio 4
Naga Munchetty – BBC Radio 5 Live
Jeremy Vine – BBC Radio 2
TalkRadio
LBC
Times Radio
BBC Radio London

SPECIALIST TITLES

Specialist titles are great to pitch if you operate in a particular niche. Below is an idea of some specialist titles that may appeal to you, but do research into the most influential ones in your industry. Sites like The Drum and Campaign cover marketing news, whereas Raconteur creates content for C-Suite executives and leaders, and the *Jewish Chronicle* is a newspaper for Jewish interest stories.

Raconteur
Campaign
The Drum
Courier
Freelancer Magazine
The Week
The Spectator
The Gentlewoman
Journalism.co.uk
Jewish Chronicle
The London Review of Books
The World of Interiors
Hypebeast

ORGANISATIONS WITH EDITORIAL

Newspapers and magazines are one route for press, but don't overlook other places where you may be able to spread the word about your work. Enterprise Nation is an organisation for small businesses that allows you to set yourself up as a blogger on their site and self-publish content. Private members club for women, the AllBright, has a magazine called *The Edit* where they publish women's interest stories. Found & Flourish is another business collective with an editorial platform attached. You may also want to self-publish on sites such as Medium and Substack, this can be another great way to build your public profile online.

Enterprise Nation
AllBright – *The Edit*
The Stack World
The Coven

Found & Flourish
EveryWoman
Medium
Substack

CASE STUDY:
JO CARR ON HOW TO CREATE AN OBJECTIVES-DRIVEN PR STRATEGY

Jo Carr is a PR expert and co-founder of Hope&Glory PR, a creative PR agency with clients including IKEA, Airbnb and Virgin Active. Here she shares her insights on what creates a successful PR strategy:

Name: Jo Carr
Age: 53
Job title: Co-founder and chief client officer, Hope&Glory PR

What makes a strong, objectives-driven PR strategy?
I think with anything in life the trick is to keep it simple. Too often, a brief can have a number of different and sometimes opposing objectives and that can lead to complexity and confusion. The best PR strategies and campaigns are single-minded in their approach and memorable because they did one thing very well.

When it comes to setting objectives for the campaign, what kind of things should you be considering?
There are numerous different reasons why you might want to kick off a PR campaign. You might want to influence behaviour or lobby for change; you may want to change public opinion or repair a reputation; or you might want to build awareness that will help your sales effort. In the world of consumer PR that I operate in, our role is mostly helping brands build awareness and fame that leads to an enhanced reputation and ultimately

contributes to the bottom line: more sales or bums on seats. It's all about finding interesting ways to get talked about so your brand or service is front of mind.

What are some realistic goals you set for your clients in campaigns?

The goals we commonly set are around raising awareness or ensuring a brand is remaining relevant to its audience, and hence is forging a connection with them.

What have you found to be successful in pitching during the pandemic?

Human interest stories are always a winner. Especially if they involve overcoming a struggle in a David versus Goliath way, or flip a well-known convention such as man bites dog. That's what makes them newsworthy. At the start of the pandemic, stories that told how brands were contributing to the greater good landed well: how brands were contributing to the national effort to fight Covid. That might have been retailers prioritising or rewarding NHS workers or campaigns tackling loneliness or the mental-health pandemic. Stories with a higher purpose won the war for attention. That then gave way to lighter, more entertaining content as the public craved some frivolity and to find light in an otherwise dark place.

Are there any stories or trends that have surprised you in the last few years?

The thing to remember is that stories and trends tend to be cyclical. They tend to come around again with relative frequency. The media always love to be able to mention emerging social channels or platforms. Back in the day, incorporating Twitter or Instagram into a story gave it more traction and relevance. The same principle applies now but the platforms have changed, which is why we see more stories now mentioning TikTok or NFTs. Prepare to hear and read more about the Metaverse than ever before.

Any advice for start-ups on how to get PR?

It really depends on what it is that you are selling. If you have a product or a service to push, there are several things you might consider. You may wish to gift it to relevant media or influencers to trial or experience, although you can't control how they write it up or whether they have a favourable opinion. That's why it's so powerful or potent if a third party does endorse it (and this is where PR has the edge over advertising in terms of credibility). You may choose to promote the brand by telling the story of how it was founded and profiling the individuals behind the business. This is typically aimed at trade media or business media whose readers are interested in the brand genesis story. Another route is to be an activist, and land on an issue or cause that resonates with your audience. The trick with that route is to ensure what you say and what you do are completely joined up. For example, don't call for female empowerment or levelling up if your board is all male. You need to walk the talk.

And a final point on this, don't drink the kool-aid. A good PR will be the cynic in the room. Just because you think your business is the bee's knees, don't expect others to feel the same.

How can you measure the success of your PR campaign?

This is the million-dollar question. It's not easy and I wish there was a golden bullet. We usually measure what we call outputs, out-takes and outcome. The outputs are the direct results of the campaign itself, for example an influencer post or a piece of online news coverage, a picture of your product or service in a print publication or a mention in a journalist opinion piece. We then measure the out-takes, which is inherently a campaign's 'talkability' and propensity for a message to spread. We might do this via social metrics, circulation and reach figures of magazines and online news sites. What has the audience done with the initial message it received – has it been passed on? But it's not enough to get a story out and trending, what change in behaviour has it prompted? That's when we might review sales figures (or propensity to buy), opinion polls, hits to websites or changes in behaviour, all of which we call outcomes.

Hope&Glory PR
https://www.hopeandglorypr.com/

WORKBOOK: CREATING YOUR OBJECTIVES-DRIVEN PR PLAN

It's time to get building your own PR plan. Grab a pen and paper and start thinking about the strategy you're going to put in place for your PR campaign:

1. What are the three key objectives of your PR plan?

2. What are the main titles you're going to pitch?

3. What will be the most effective route for publicity for your business right now?

4. What stands out to you from this chapter about creating PR opportunities?

5. What are three actions you can take this week to get started?

CHAPTER THREE

How to Secure
Media Opportunities

Finding high-quality media opportunities is perhaps one of the hardest aspects of any PR strategy, so in this chapter I'm going to guide you through finding media opportunities and, more importantly, securing them.

I'll explain what journalists are really looking for when they are working on a story and how you can give yourself the best chance of getting featured. It's one thing to find an opportunity, it's another to pitch yourself successfully to boost your chance of coverage.

Getting opportunities can be hard when you don't know where to start, so let's begin by breaking down the different routes for finding media opportunities, and then I'll share some top tips for each from the journalist's perspective. Beyond this, I'd also like to look at creating your own opportunities, which is a different skillset itself and feeds into the visibility blueprint we'll look at in the next chapter as a founder. Sometimes, the best ways to get opportunities is to make your own, and I've got lots of ideas for how you can do that.

Let's start by looking at ways to find media opportunities for you and your business.

FIVE WAYS TO FIND MEDIA OPPORTUNITIES

I don't believe that media should be a 'pay to play' world and if you don't want to stretch to the high cost of a PR agency, there are lots of free and low-cost ways to find media opportunities yourself:

1. SUBSCRIBE TO MEDIA ALERT SERVICES

There are lots of great databases that journalists use when writing a story – you can sign up for many of these alert services for free and you'll get notified via email when a journalist is looking for experts, case studies or commentary for a feature. Editorielle is a fantastic newsletter that collates the best journalist requests from social media in the day into one place so you can easily find opportunities and pitch in. The ones I personally use the most when working on a story are as follows:

➡ ResponseSource
➡ Cision
➡ Journolink
➡ Editorielle
➡ Press Plugs

You can sign up for alerts on their respective websites. There are also a few PR-focused Facebook groups that I use when looking for case studies quickly. The ones I use most are:

➡ Lightbulb
➡ PR for the People

Remember to be quick to respond when finding media opportunities on these alert services! Digital media is very fast-moving and I'd normally file a story a few hours after first working on it, so you need to be speedy with pitching to be included. Make sure you have all your press materials to hand so that you can respond quickly with all the relevant information.

2. CHECK #JOURNOREQUESTS
The #journorequests hashtag on Twitter can be a great way to find opportunities, although you'll have to sift through to find good ones. If you don't know, this hashtag is used when a journalist is working on a story and needs support on it. It's also fast-moving, so I wouldn't recommend responding to anything that's more than two hours old as the story has probably been filed already. Often a

journalist will expect you to reply privately on Twitter to their request, so it's good to be succinct when responding – have a few lines prepared about yourself, a snappy elevator pitch, and highlight your relevancy and connection to the story or subject matter.

I often use this hashtag as a way of working out who's working where – journalists are often moving roles and titles, so it can be a useful way of following relevant people and keeping track of who's writing for which publications. I'd recommend creating your own Excel spreadsheet with contacts so you can keep tabs on who are the right people to pitch at different publications.

3. JOIN A PR MEMBERSHIP
In recent years, a new hybrid form of PR agency has evolved: the PR membership is a much lower cost option to traditional agencies that gives you a helping hand for your PR strategy. Many of these PR memberships offer monthly trainings, live Q&As with journalists, resources and contacts to support your PR plan – they basically give you the basis you need for pitching, but don't do the actual work itself. This can be a really great way to have some support in your PR plan but without the overheads of an agency and the opportunity to hone your own pitching skills.

There are quite a few PR memberships to choose from. In the UK, my personal favourites are:

⇨　Media Matchmaker
⇨　PR for the People
⇨　Amanda PR

4. BUILD A NETWORK OF JOURNALISTS
Often you won't hear about a story that you'd be perfect for until it's too late. There are lots of opportunities to get into the press that simply don't advertise themselves online, but happen through word of mouth, quick phone calls and last-minute deadlines. The only way you're going to hear about these opportunities is by having a real and genuine relationship with a journalist, so think about how

you can build personal connections. It starts with following the right people online, but then you want to take the relationship off-line and find ways to connect and deepen those relationships in real life.

Network is so important to your PR plan – the bigger the network, the more opportunities will come your way.

We'll look at building rapport with journalists in a later chapter, but, for now, just take note of how important it is to focus on building authentic relationships off-screen and make that a priority within your PR plan.

5. COLD-PITCH YOURSELF

You don't always have to wait for the perfect opportunity to get yourself in the media – cold-pitching is very much the vibe of the industry and if you think you have a great story to tell, then pitch yourself in. Do your research on the right publication, and make things snappy and succinct.

TOP TIPS:
RESPONDING TO #JOURNOREQUESTS

⇨ Don't use #journorequests as a way of pursuing your own agenda. Make sure your pitch is genuinely relevant to what they are writing about.

⇨ Shoot your shot but do it quickly. Don't hesitate when replying or think too long about the copy; just reach out, be friendly and personable.

⇨ Have your press kit ready, so if you are successful, you have all the relevant press materials to hand.

CASE STUDY:
NAOMI WHITE ON FINDING A PRESS HOOK

Naomi White is a PR coach and consultant and founder of Naomi White Communications. Over the past decade, she has built up an impressive portfolio representing some of the health and wellness industries' most prestigious brands, from pioneering health-tech to well-known personal-profiling clients. Here are her insights on how to find a press 'hook' for your story:

Name: Naomi White
Age: 31
Job title: PR coach and consultant

What makes a great press hook?
There are a few key things that make a great press hook in my eyes:

Timely – think about what is happening in the wider world and whether your pitch is the right pitch, right now. For example, when the pandemic hit a lot of health and wellness brands with bricks and mortar studios became irrelevant to people, unless they were able to pivot and create at-home/online content, which is something people could engage with at that time.

Relevant – firstly do your research and select the right publications to pitch to. Think about your target market, does it match that of the publication's readership? Then think about whether the idea you're pitching is relevant to that readership too.

Solves a problem or inspires the publication's readership – is your pitch going to captivate their readership? Often what journalists are looking for are solutions to people's problems. For example, a large proportion of the population struggle with sleep – can you create tips to help combat insomnia? Or perhaps you're launching a new product or app in the sleep space that will help solve sleep problems – this is what journalists want to hear about. Similarly, if you have an inspiring story that could help others, for example, providing business tips as to how you became an entrepreneur is an angle that will entice a readership to buy a magazine, newspaper or read an online article.

What's your golden rule when it comes to pitching the press?

Go into meetings with a loose agenda of what coverage you would like to achieve (I often go into meetings without an expectation of coverage at all). Sometimes the best coverage comes because of building a relationship and doesn't always happen immediately. Keep those relationships going even when it's not resulting in coverage as you never know where it may lead. The relationships you establish at a lower level may one day become editor status and extremely valuable, or they may move to a more sought-after publication.

When building a PR strategy, what factors do you consider?

There are some key factors to consider:

PR focus – what are you promoting month by month? For example, product launches, campaigns or seasonal offers.

What are you pitching in relation to your PR focus? Such as a review of a product, an event listings or a trip.

Relevant dates – national days are often covered by the press and can be a great way to gain coverage. However, be conscious to only pick the dates that are truly relevant to your brand and create a unique pitch idea to break through the noise of many other brands looking to also use national dates to their advantage.

Call to action – for a brand this is the most important part. What are you looking to achieve? How are you going to achieve this? Where are you driving traffic to?

In the health and well-being space, what questions should you be asking yourself about whether it's a good story?
These are the questions I often ask myself when pitching:

Is your brand keeping up with demands of what consumers are looking for? For example, sustainability is a hot topic right now and will be for many years to come. What is your brand doing in this space to be more sustainable? Could you potentially use this as your hook?

Are you pitching in line with the latest trends? Have a look at the future trends in your industry through sites such as Welltodo.

Is the angle you're pitching new and innovative? Or has it been heavily covered before? If it has, it's unlikely you'll break through the noise and get featured.

Are you being tone deaf as to what consumers want to hear about just because you want to promote your brand? Think about whether your narrative is going to be of interest to consumers given what's happening in your industry at that given time. For example, if weight loss is being heavily covered as a 'taboo' subject in January, how can you create a more positive narrative around this that consumers will be excited and inspired by?

How can an entrepreneur or founder get press? What are your tips for helping yourself get publicity?
My four gold rules are:

1. Build a brand for yourself that journalists want to feature – think about what makes you unique?

2. Make sure you have professional profile imagery – this was

a game changer for my PR agency and coaching business and can not only be used for pitching purposes but also for your website and social media.

3. Be visible on social media – a lot of journalists use social media to research stories, especially first-person pieces. Social media is also a great way to connect and build relationships with new journalists.

4. Think about how you can help their readership. Being featured in a media publication is a value exchange between you and the publication; by being featured you're gaining a huge amount of exposure, so in return you have to offer value back in the form of, for example, an inspiring story or tips to help others.

Have you got any advice on putting on press events?

⇨ If you're going to host an event, host it well. Think about the experience an attendee will go through from start to finish. If you were in their shoes would this event be one that you'll love and remember?

⇨ Think about how your event is going to entice journalists and influencers to attend. If you can afford to have a well-known industry figure as part of the event, perhaps they could host a panel and/or speak with press for an interview opportunity; this is a great way to entice a journalist to attend and also gives them a way to feature your brand.

⇨ Research what events other brands have hosted recently and see what gained traction and what didn't. Take inspiration.

⇨ If you're going to provide a goodie bag, make it a *great* goodie bag or don't do one at all.

⇨ Create a great opportunity for attendees to capture social content – for example, a flower wall, branded board, etc.

Then make it clear as to how they can tag you on social media (social handle, hashtags, etc).

⇨ Don't expect coverage off the back of your event unless you're giving them a reason to feature you. For example, showcasing a new product launch or having talent involved as mentioned above.

What do events look like in a post-pandemic world? Is there any way to future-proof your events?

The pandemic saw a huge rise in online events and I don't think this will change any time soon; if anything, online events are a blessing in disguise for brands and attendees. For brands it often costs less to host an online event and for press it's more convenient. London Fashion Week has transitioned from in-person catwalks to online, and this has saved fashion and beauty journalists a lot of time in travel and enables them to access more events than they would be able to attend in person – a win-win situation. In terms of future-proofing your events, no one was ever going to predict the global pandemic and the impact it has had on events, but I think people have learnt to now have a contingency plan in place. You can't predict the future but you can be prepared to make the best out of a bad situation.

How important is social media in building a PR strategy?

Social media is very important if you want to remain at the forefront of consumers' minds. Everyone of every age is on social media (even my granny!), whether that be Facebook, Twitter, Instagram or TikTok. The important element for brands to think about is where their ideal client or customer is more active, and then concentrate on that platform and making their social media presence the best it can be to captivate their target market.

Naomi White Communications
https://www.naomiwhitecommunications.com/

FIVE WAYS TO CREATE YOUR OWN MEDIA OPPORTUNITIES

A successful PR plan should include a rich mix of different ways to find and create your own opportunities – you can't always expect things to land in your lap and there's lots you can do to support yourself in getting media opportunities.

Below are some ideas for daily, monthly and annual activities you can do to create your own opportunities. These work well alongside some of the visibility-raising actions that we'll look at in the next chapter.

1. READ THE NEWS EVERY DAY

Perhaps this seems like a basic one, but I'm often surprised by how little people actually read the news while trying to build a PR plan.

If you want to be part of the news, you need to know what's going on in the news. Simple.

So, start by taking an interest in the news cycle and what's happening in your industry and the wider world around you. If you're going to be strategic about your news consumption, I would set up Google Keywords for relevant keywords in your industry or line of work, so you can get notified by email daily when there are news stories that are particularly relevant to you. I'd also recommend doing this for your own name or business name, so if you do get any publicity, you won't miss it.

This is a good strategy for working out who the relevant writers and journalists for your niche are. You can keep tabs on the articles they write, follow them on social media and engage with their work more deeply. Actually reading the publications you want to get featured in is the first step to getting coverage. Be a reader, if you want to be a feature.

Beyond this, I would get into the habit of responding and reacting to the news – whether that's writing a LinkedIn post in response to a news story, an Instagram caption or Twitter thread. Be part of the conversation.

By adding something new, you're making yourself more relevant and interesting to journalists and placing yourself within the news cycle in your own way. This is something that journalists will take note of, and I would get in the habit of responding to two to three news stories a week on your social media platforms. It also sets you up for writing opinion pieces or giving first-person insights into a topic – it's good to have an opinion and show personality, as it increases your press-worthiness.

2. TAKE NOTE OF NATIONAL AWARENESS DAYS

Awareness days can be a great press hook for a story and it's always good to plan ahead to see what's coming up and whether you can create an interesting press story that links to the topic. Some ideas of awareness days to take note of:

⇨ Valentine's Day
⇨ International Women's Day
⇨ Father's Day and Mother's Day
⇨ Earth Day
⇨ Christmas Day

Be mindful of not shoehorning or forcing a story into one of these days, however – it's better to be authentic and bespoke in your approach. That might mean creating a special offering for Father's Day or putting on an event for International Women's Day. Whatever it is, make sure it's genuinely relevant to the day itself.

Also, it's worth noting that journalists will be looking for experts for commentary around different times of the year. For example, in January, there will be lots of interest around health and well-being content, whereas in the summer it might be travel experts needed, or at Christmas time retail experts. To some extent you can predict when there's going to be the most interest in your line of work and so set yourself up in a good position for those opportunities at the time.

3. DEVELOP YOUR WRITING SKILLS

I genuinely think one of the best ways to get publicity is by positioning yourself as a writer, rather than expecting the journalist to write about you. It's a different route to doing things than traditional PR and not something an agency will normally tell you to do, but if you want to set yourself up as a thought-leader in your industry, get writing!

You can write features, opinion pieces, how-to style articles or trend-led prediction pieces. You can start by publishing these on your own website or blog, and once they've gained some traction, start pitching around for other places to write for. Websites like Huffpost, Metro and iNews often take new writers who haven't been published before, so don't let lack of experience hold you back.

By developing your writing skills, you'll create buzz and attract PR opportunities. Writing for magazines is a great way to build profile, and we'll look in a later chapter about how you can get inspiration for stories. If you're not a confident writer, take a short course and learn. There are lots of great online courses and, in the UK, CityLit does an affordable writing for magazines short course.

4. APPLY FOR AWARDS

Awards are another great way to build your profile and generate press opportunities, and lots of them are free to enter. The more you grow your profile, the more press opportunities will come to you.

Awards are a natural super-charge for your career – journalists will often look at the list of award nominees, shortlists and winners when looking for people to profile or interview for stories. And if you win an award, the organiser will often support you with their own PR efforts. If you want to be an expert in your field, winning an award will go a long way to supporting that goal.

Aim to apply for a couple of awards every year and take time to thoroughly craft an application. Here are a few high-profile awards that it might be worth entering, although it's also worth researching the most prominent ones in your industry:

⇨ The Great British Entrepreneur Awards
⇨ The British Business Awards

⇨ StartUp Britain
⇨ WeAreTheCity Rising Star Awards
⇨ Everywoman Awards

5. APPLY FOR HIGH-PROFILE LISTS

There's a lot to be said for getting featured on some high-profile, 'ones to watch' lists, and we often forget that we can put ourselves forward for these opportunities; you don't have to be selected independently by the publisher for them.

Forbes 30 Under 30 is the classic one that lots of people know and has instant recognition factor, but if (like me!) you've passed the age bracket for this, there are lots of other great lists to be included on. Many of them have application forms and deadlines shared online, so do include these in your PR strategy when planning for the year.

Here's an overview of some websites that publish industry-specific 'ones to watch' lists you might want to apply for or reach out to the editors about:

⇨ Enterprise Nation
⇨ The Drum
⇨ *Marie Claire*
⇨ *Business Insider*
⇨ Cision
⇨ Vuelio

6. SPEND AN HOUR PITCHING EVERY DAY

This might seem obvious, but if you don't put the time in, you won't get results. If you can carve out an hour every morning for some of these profile-raising activities, it will do wonders for your PR momentum.

I'd recommend spending an hour a day pitching stories to different publications – this might be in response to a news story that's just broken (again, remember the importance of relevancy), reaching out to journalists to go for coffee, or coming up with story ideas that you could publish on your platforms.

To create media opportunities, you must begin by becoming confident producing your own content. Get in the habit of writing pitches, getting confident about the process of firing off emails and trying to build warm leads. The more you send out, the more chances you'll have of getting coverage.

TOP TIP:
BE THE NEWS

My final top tip on getting media coverage is: sometimes to get into the news, you have to *be* the news first. We often think we need to hang off a news story, but what if you reframe things – what if you're the news story itself? Don't be afraid of making a splash. Perhaps you can employ some guerrilla marketing tactics to launch a new product or service, create an interesting press drop of goodies for journalists, or invest in consumer research that will complement your story. Don't be afraid to be bold and stand out.

CASE STUDY:
PHIL DAVE ON HOW TO GET FEATURED ON THE RADIO

Phil Dave is weekend content editor for TalkTV, and has previously worked as a producer on the BBC and TalkRadio. Here, he shares his thoughts on how you can get featured on the radio:

Name: Phil Dave
Job title: Weekend content editor at TalkTV

What do you think makes a great story for radio? What really catches your eye?
The answer is two-fold: the first part is in the email and press release itself. Make it stand out. If it's just a load of text, it's

probably going to get lost in a sea of emails. Whereas if there are some different fonts, maybe some striking images and a bit of colour to it, it's much more likely to get noticed. The second part is to make it relatable. It's much more likely to resonate if it's something Jo Public can connect with, for example the story of an individual rather than the story of a company or product. Everyone loves an underdog, someone who's risen against the odds.

What's the best way for people to approach you to get featured on the radio?
Peg it to something, don't just approach a producer with a 'great story', everyone thinks their stories are great – otherwise why bother. It's much better if you can hook it to a story that is in the news. This isn't always possible but it does increase the chances as it justifies why that producer has booked them. Of course, if it's actually ground-breaking, then you could be the one to set the news agenda.

What are some questions you should ask yourself before pitching your story to a radio producer?

⇨ Would I listen to what this person has to say? Am I genuinely interested? If not, why would I expect other people to be?

⇨ Is it something that could go viral? Keeping in mind what social media seems to love in this day and age, is it something I could see catching on? (This is not essential but it helps.)

⇨ Will this make a solid ten-minute slot or would it start to run dry after just one question? If the answer is it will run dry, then maybe it needs a bit of padding out.

How do you think getting featured on the radio differs from other types of media?

It's the one true chance at a genuine conversation around your story. In television there are far more time constraints, which usually means it's all pre-arranged questions and answers. On social media, it's a flash in the pan, thirty to sixty seconds maximum, otherwise people lose interest. On radio, it's the heart of a segment, its focus is entirely on the story as there's no visual stimulation to distract. It's the best way to get a message out there both expressively and subliminally.

What advice would you give someone who wanted to get their business or brand featured on the radio and why?

People pay for adverts, if you want to 'feature' on radio then make sure it is a feature and not a commercial in disguise. Trust that the presenter you'd be working with is experienced enough to give you ample opportunity to talk about your brand or business without the need for commercial speak. No one wants to hear the words 'highly competitive' or 'really great value'. Just have a conversation and most listeners are intuitive enough to pick up on the appeal of a brand or business without the need to sell it to them. Otherwise, if a listener thinks something is turning into a ten-minute infomercial, they're more than likely to zone out.

Follow Phil Dave on Twitter
https://twitter.com/mrphildave

WORKBOOK: FINDING MEDIA OPPORTUNITIES FOR YOUR BUSINESS

Now we've explored how to get media opportunities, it's time to get clear on how you're personally going to pursue press opportunities for your business. Let's dive into some questions to help you build the big picture:

1. What daily habits can you commit to for finding media opportunities?

2. Which services or memberships might you like to join?

3. What areas of weakness do you need to remedy to create more opportunities for yourself?

4. What platform excites you most for finding opportunities?

5. In what ways do you think you can stand out with your PR plan?

CHAPTER FOUR

How to Create a Visibility Blueprint as a Founder

One of the biggest shifts I've seen in the last few years in the media landscape is the move from business to personal PR – where the focus is on the individual behind the business and 'personal brand'. We've seen this term banded around a lot within the entrepreneurship world, but what actually makes an effective personal brand, and how can you create one?

Personal brand, to me, means having an identity and (good) reputation that precedes you. It can mean your work fits into a particular niche – being known for something specific within your industry – although having a niche isn't necessary to build a personal brand. Personal brand in recent years has often centred around aesthetics, but to me it's more than wearing the same colour consistently (think Steve Jobs in his uniform of black turtlenecks) or having a picture-perfect Instagram profile – it's about having a streamlined brand and vision within your work, having a clear idea of who you're talking to and why. Personal brand, at its heart, is about consistency – of message, content and direction.

There's certainly a correlation between a strong personal brand and getting publicity as a founder, and in this chapter, I'm going to give you some insights into how founders, entrepreneurs and experts can build their potential to gain publicity. Making yourself press-worthy as a founder is about being strategic, and in my experience, there are some key things that need to happen to put yourself in the position to get media opportunities. These are insights I've learnt in my ten-plus years as an entrepreneur in the media world – secrets people rarely share, and I'm excited to reveal them to you in this chapter.

So, let's dive into how you can get highly visible as a founder, make yourself attractive to the media and allow a flow of press requests to come your way.

WHAT IS VISIBILITY AND WHY DOES IT MATTER?

Firstly, I want to look at what we mean by visibility and how it can be applied to your work. When defining visibility, there are some key elements to getting highly visible as a founder:

VISIBILITY IS . . . EXPERTISE

Want to get visible? Start by focusing on what your unique expertise is.

Visibility, for me, is about creating connection – it's about an audience or brands connecting your work to certain topics and being recognised for your work. For example, you might be a nutritionist who specialises in supporting women's health – good visibility would mean that an audience quickly and easily connect your work with women's health, and you're invited to speak, write and inform on the topic in the press. Being 'visible' means you're the go-to founder for commentary and someone the press deems a reliable source of expertise and insights on a topic.

Knowing what your personal expertise is is the building block for gaining visibility as a founder.

It's always valuable to try to narrow down that expertise as much as possible – from a press perspective, it's better not to be a jack of all trades and the more specific you can be on your 'zone of genius', the greater chance you'll have of standing out from other experts. This doesn't mean, however, that your expertise must always stay the same; as your career progresses, you can invite new topics in or focus on emerging areas of interest, but as a starting point, it's good to have a clearly defined area of expertise.

VISIBILITY IS . . . LEADERSHIP

Want to get more visible? Start thinking of yourself as a thought leader in your industry. What this means, in basic terms, is leading the charge with innovation, discussion and debate within your industry. It means staying on top of the news, especially stories that directly affect your work or industry, and making yourself part of the conversation.

There are lots of ways you can do this, from using LinkedIn strategically to position yourself as a thought-leader by sharing insights and commentary around the news, to building a community on Instagram that sets you up as a person of note within your industry and network. Social media plays a valuable part in positioning yourself as a thought-leader, and if this is a route you want to explore, you'll have to get strategic about the kind of stories and content you're sharing online so that they align with your goals as a brand founder.

VISIBILITY IS . . . RECOGNITION

This can mean many things depending on your industry, but I would say one of the signs that you're gathering visibility as a founder is increasing recognition for work. Recognition can take many forms. It might mean receiving awards, being featured on 'ones to watch' lists in your industry or simply getting more inbound clients. Recognition is a self-fulfilling thing; the more you're recognised for your work, the more press interest you'll get. Work on landing those first few pieces of coverage, and you'll find everything starts to flow more easily.

VISIBILITY IS . . . PUBLICITY

Why does visibility matter? Visibility is a great way to attract press – if you have the social-media proof of making waves in your industry and building a community around your work, the more attractive you appear to a journalist. Boosting your visibility makes you more press-worthy – the work you do for yourself on building a personal brand is something journalists really take note of and helps in ways you don't realise.

Visibility means you're more likely to be written about in the press and feature regularly on TV and radio. This can happen incrementally, but it's good to keep track of your personal momentum and see if you're steadily getting invited for new opportunities in the press. If you're not, it's worth going back to the drawing board with your 'visibility blueprint' (which we'll work on in this chapter) and seeing where things can be refined.

VISIBILITY IS . . . PARTNERSHIPS

One of the key benefits of getting visible as a founder is you'll naturally attract partnerships that align with your own brand. It's something you don't even have to work for, it will just happen when you're known for something – and that way, other companies will reach out to you, as your work precedes you. That clarity of your 'why' will help the right kind of partnerships come your way (although you must be savvy about what you accept and align with). Get clear on your personal expertise and content, and the right people will find your work.

VISIBILITY IS . . . FLOW

I want an easy life in my business. I want opportunities to come my way and I don't want to constantly hustle to make those happen – I want to spend less time doing press outreach, and more time focusing on income and growth in my business.

People say networking is key for business, but personally I've found the most effective networking tool – far better than attending networking events – is focusing efforts on building your own profile. Build your own brand, and then you won't even need to network – people, opportunities and connections will all come to you. That's the strongest form of networking you can do. Build your own network by building your own brand.

So, if you want more flow in your business and for work to feel less like work, start by making yourself visible as a founder.

BUILDING A VISIBILITY BLUEPRINT

So, now we've looked at what visibility is and why it matters as a founder, let's dive into how you can go about building your own visibility blueprint.

For this, I'd like you to consider both online and offline efforts to build visibility. During the pandemic, we tended to prioritise online opportunities (naturally, as virtual activities are a safer bet), but as we emerge out of the pandemic, I think it's important to re-prioritise offline activities that can build your brand. A balanced mix of online and offline efforts will help you build a strong personal brand – don't hide away just doing online activities, as connecting face to face is still very important.

EXERCISE: **UNDERSTANDING YOUR VISIBILITY WHY**

Before we launch into how to build visibility, I want you to take a moment and consider *why* you want to do it. Grab a pen and paper and answer these questions in your own time:

- What do you want to be known for? And why does that matter?
- What is your expertise?
- What do you have access to that other people don't?
- What makes you stand out in your industry?
- What platforms are your audience hanging out on online?
- How do you want to position yourself within your industry?
- What social media platforms will support your objectives best?

Now, let's look at the details. Here's a checklist of visibility-building activities to consider, and then we're going to deep-dive into how you maximise and attract them:

ONLINE	OFFLINE
⇨ Social media	⇨ Events
⇨ Video content	⇨ Networking
⇨ Online media	⇨ Public speaking
⇨ Working with influencers	⇨ Podcasts
	⇨ Print and broadcast media
	⇨ Books

VISIBILITY BLUEPRINT: ONLINE

Want to boost your visibility online? Here's some things to consider:

SOCIAL MEDIA

As a founder, one of the most effective things you can do to build your visibility is get savvy about how you use social media. Social media can really complement your PR plan and boost your profile, but some strategy is required to determine which platforms and content to focus on.

So, firstly, on a content strategy for social media, here's the way I would recommend doing things:

⇨ Pick three platforms to focus on
⇨ Pick three 'content pillars'
⇨ Experiment with a cadence that works for you
⇨ Stick at a strategy for at least six weeks before tweaking

There's no need to be across every social media platform; far better to do a few better than spreading yourself too thin across multiple platforms. Same goes for having too many accounts: it's better to have a main account that you're able to consistently update. Social media shouldn't be too draining or time-consuming, but something instead that you find ease and flow with. And, most importantly, something that you enjoy using.

Figure out which platforms are best for your business. LinkedIn is very effective for professional development. Instagram is great for lifestyle businesses. TikTok can be incredible if you have a product business. If you're an entrepreneur with a story to tell, YouTube might be the place you want to do that. I'm giving you permission to not be everywhere – again, it's about being strategic about what is going to be the most effective route to achieving your goals.

If you do have the time, I'd always recommend having a personal Instagram account, as well as one for your business, where you can show the behind-the-scenes of your work and take people on a journey with you. Personal accounts are a great way to build relationships with your audience and show some personality and flair.

When it comes to the actual content, the easiest way to do things is pick three core content pillars of things you want to talk about – and then innovate within them. The more specific the better, as this will help you create regular content with ease. For example, my three content pillars are entrepreneurship, empowerment and coaching. This sits within an overall umbrella of business leadership but helps me create more tailored content towards my niche: women entrepreneurs and self-employed individuals.

PR SUCCESS STORY:
TANYA ROBERTSON, FOUNDER OF WOMANHOOD

Throughout the book, we'll be sharing success stories from business owners who have seen great results through PR. Here, we hear from Tanya Robertson, founder of womanhood, on her PR journey:

Name: Tanya Robertson
Age: 28
Job title: Founder, womanhood

How impactful has PR been to your business?
From brand awareness to direct sales, to top funnel customer

acquisition, the power of PR for womanhood has been instrumental in its early growth.

We've recognised from the beginning that PR for us isn't about quick wins, it is part of a longer-term plan to establish womanhood and build a consistent picture of the brand. We predominately use publicity as a part of our top funnel activity to introduce new potential customers into our community. In some instances, it may relate to sales straightaway, but in others it brings our brand into people's awareness and allows us to build a relationship with them over time.

What benefit has the business received from getting press?

Publicity has been a piece of the jigsaw puzzle for womanhood, tying together various digital marketing activations and brand profile building.

Past the obvious benefits of earned media, PR has had a positive impact across our SEO working simultaneously to amplify campaign results. Similarly, press coverage has boosted our paid search and social ads on a retargeting level, allowing us to re-engage with audiences that may have discovered us from something in the press and develop the narrative past the initial interaction they've had with the brand.

What has helped you get press coverage?

As womanhood is primarily a retailer, we lean on our brand narrative and proposition to stand apart. Given the lingerie market is typically oversaturated with the male gaze and overtly sexy skimpy underwear, we stand apart by catering to the female gaze and providing solutions to customers looking to dress for themselves rather than someone else. Building our story around our differences not only allows us to gain recognition, it means we stand apart through our visual representation, brands, styles and sizes.

Any tips for working with the media and building relationships?

Be consistent, persistent and act on relevant moments, stories and calendar events that are relevant to your brand.

Put your brand and your team forward for any and all opportunities that come your way and, where possible, try to meet with journalists in person to build relationships past emails.

What are some of the short-term and long-term benefits you've had from press coverage?

Without a doubt the most impactful piece of coverage we had was from a BBC CEO Secrets interview, where I discussed the problem of raising investment as a sole female founder, especially when talking about boobs and bras to a traditionally male investor audience. We were in the midst of our seed round and traction was building at a steady rate, but nothing could have prepared us for the change that happened literally overnight.

In typical fashion we didn't know specifics of which part of the interview they'd be using, or when it would come out. Where I was originally having to cold call, knock on doors, trying any means to get an in, suddenly investors were coming to us and asking to be a part of our investment round. That day was one of the most memorable in womanhood's history. There was nothing to do except watch the stream of emails, calls, LinkedIn messages and social comments of thousands of people discovering us overnight, and crucially at that time, potential investors wanting to be involved. womanhood would undoubtably be in a different position today if it wasn't for that interview.

What advice would you give start-ups wanting to get press coverage?

Build the essentials to have ready at any point: product imagery, price information, press releases, founder images, lookbooks.

Your assets are your biggest tool, especially in the early days.

If you're not regularly launching new products, which is one of the easiest ways to gain PR coverage, look to your data to build a news story. Providing insights and trends is a great way to cut through in the beginning. It will help paint a picture of your brand past the products.

Little actions can also go a long way – find relevant journalists on Instagram and build relationships with them away from email. Sometimes it's easier to catch someone's attention with content than it is with pitch emails.

Where possible get your products in front of the press. Whether it's through gifting, organising press meetings or sending samples to shoots, make sure you're available and able to send items that can easily help you achieve greater coverage.

Lastly, it's important to remember that PR results aren't instant. They take time, effort and energy. Building relationships with journalists can be a lengthy process but it will ultimately be worth it.

What's in store for your business in the next twelve months?

Our primary focuses for the next year is continuing building out our collection of female-founded brands, educating our community on fit, breast and body shapes through innovative technology, and helping everyone who buys from womanhood to feel great in their lingerie. We have several announcements in the next year that we can't wait to share!

womanhood
https://womanhood.shop/

Checklist: Social Media Must-Dos

Need a quick reminder of best practice for social?
Here's a checklist of things to consider for your social feeds:

⇨ Talking to camera
⇨ Regular Instagram, TikTok or LinkedIn Lives
⇨ Behind-the-scenes content
⇨ Use Instagram 'Story' features
⇨ Use LinkedIn strategically
⇨ Consistency over perfection

Super-charged Social – Quick Tips for Founders

Show your face – visibility is all about being seen. How much are you letting your audience really see you? It's normal to be nervous talking to camera – it's the number one thing I hear when I coach one-to-one on PR. But showing up online is important, and it's about more than having a physical presence – it's one of the best ways to build connection and trust with your audience, by showing up as your full self.

I know talking to camera can feel daunting at first, but you'll quickly get over the fear the more you do it and in time you will forget that it can feel a little odd. Putting your face to camera, whether that's video content, Instagram Lives or starting a YouTube channel, is beneficial for every founder who wants to get more visible.

Do IG Lives – We can get a little meticulous when it comes to content creation, but don't overthink it – it's great to be more off-the-cuff to build connection with your audience. Instagram Lives are, again, nerve-wracking to start with but can be so helpful as a founder to boost your visibility. Try to get into the habit of a weekly Live and make it a regular series.

Lives are also a great way to collaborate with other founders or individuals in your network, and position yourself as a thought-leader in your space as you're opening interesting conversations through your platform. I think around twenty minutes is the sweet spot for Lives and I've found 1 p.m. or 6 p.m. the best time to do them, when the most people are on the app and engaging with it. Don't be disheartened if lots of people don't tune in live – it's still beneficial to keep doing Lives and those numbers will grow in time. You can also save it to your profile afterwards for people to watch back, so it's an easy win for an extra piece of content for your grid.

Behind-the-scenes content – Often we want our online content to be shiny and polished, but this is not a reflection of reality, and I've found the 'messier' and more true to life my content is the more an audience connects with it – so don't be afraid of showing your whole self online. Showing the behind-the-scenes of a business and the things that haven't necessarily gone right is a valuable thing. It takes your audience on a journey with you and puts them at the heart of your business, rather than positioning them as an outsider. So, show everything – perhaps that's a personal challenge and how you've overcome it, or explaining a particular obstacle in your business and what you've done to rise to it – that journey makes content rich and interesting. Don't forget, just be you!

Use Instagram Story features – The features on the back end of Instagram are there for a reason, and they can be a great way to bring your audience into your business and make them feel part of things. Use the polls, quizzes and questions on Instagram Stories to get to know your audience. Get them involved in business decisions and include them in your day-to-day. If you're developing a new product line, ask them which options they like best; or if you're launching a new programme, speak to your audience and find out what their pain points are, and what would really serve them. Social media is meant to be about dialogue, and we can often forget that when chasing our goals with it. Remember to check in with your audience regularly and listen to them as much as you're speaking at them.

Be strategic on LinkedIn – LinkedIn is one of the best places to build online visibility as a founder. You want to be posting regularly on LinkedIn (a mixture of thought-leadership content, testimonials, industry insights and positive news) – the top 1 per cent of LinkedIn post on it every day, and if you can use it more regularly, you'll be amazed with the results. It's basically the best place on the internet to build a network with targeted results but is often neglected over the other social media platforms. Don't forget to ask for recommendations from your network also. Every time you do a speaking event, take on a coaching client or offer a service, remember to ask for a recommendation on LinkedIn; this way it can act as a multi-media CV and build your network.

Consistency over perfection – Consistency builds trust. It's one of the foundations of good social media usage and you should always aim for consistency over perfection – don't spend ages writing a caption or poring over the right image to pick, better just to post and get on with your day! Try posting at roughly the same time every day and vary the content between different styles of images, but, remember that social media is just a shop window and by posting every day, you're reminding your audience that the shop is open.

VIDEO CONTENT

Video content, again, can be very beneficial for building visibility online as a founder. You don't necessarily have to invest lots in professional filming, just try to double up and film as much content out of an opportunity as possible – even little clips that can be put together as a reel is handy. If you do find yourself with regular speaking opportunities, why not create a YouTube channel and put everything on there.

ONLINE MEDIA

If you want to get more inbound leads and visits to your website, then focus your energy on getting digital links in magazines, blogs and news sites. The goal here is to get links to your website, and this is simply a numbers game of pitching as many places as possible, to increase the chances of getting online coverage.

INFLUENCER OUTREACH

Collaborating with influencers is another great way to boost your visibility online. You must be strategic here and think about which influencers would work best for your business. You may have to put some budget aside for successful influencer collaborations, but this can be a real win if you want to spread the word about your business or service quickly.

VISIBILITY BLUEPRINT: OFFLINE

Online is not the only way to go; for a diverse and successful visibility blueprint, you need to be thinking about the actions you're going to take offline too. These actions can help build your profile in the public domain and boost your personal brand. Here are some aspects to consider:

EVENTS

Events are coming back with a bang post-pandemic and people are more keen than ever before to get out there and meet face to face. Remember to be marketing savvy at any event you do attend – have someone take photos of you and if you're giving a talk, make sure it's filmed so you can use clips on social media. If you're not getting invited on stages just yet, then make your own stage! Start your own event series or host an in-person workshop.

If you're keen to develop your speaking career, below are some tips from Lovelda Vincenzi on how to generate more speaking opportunities for yourself:

TOP TIPS
LOVELDA VINCENZI ON HOW TO GET MORE
SPEAKING OPPORTUNITIES

Lovelda Vincenzi is a global MC, host, moderator and presenter for in-person, virtual and hybrid events. She's also a speaking coach who supports female entrepreneurs to build profitable speaking businesses. Here are her top tips on generating more high-quality speaking opportunities for yourself:

Name: Lovelda Vincenzi
Age: 38
Job title: Speaker coach and international event MC

What are your five top tips on how to generate more speaking opportunities as a founder?
Founders and CEOs have a unique opportunity to use speaking in multiple ways to grow their business and create a new income stream. Not only can speaking be a PR opportunity, it can also be a marketing channel, a content creation channel or a sales channel for your business.

By using the Speaking Gig Evaluation Framework©, CEOs and founders can unlock the unlimited possibilities that speaking gives. Which begs the question, how does one generate more speaking opportunities, with ease?

Here are my five top tips to build a foundation that sets you up to become a sought-after speaker in your niche:

1. Mine Your Network
Our networks are a goldmine of untapped opportunities. The speaking world is a networked industry, a fact that often puts off those looking to tap into the market. In truth, we all have networks of people who know, like and trust us, and would happily hire us, or refer us. If they are unaware of our ambitions to get on stages, they simply won't put you forward for opportunities they come across.

I recommend anyone who wants to generate speaking opportunities to start with their current network. Make a list of people who could support your goal of getting on stage and start having conversations with them.

2. Build Your Speaker Profile

People hire who they know, like and trust, and will often use Google to verify if someone is as good as they say they are. If you are serious about getting speaking opportunities, then you need to have a digital footprint that sells your speaking services. Without it, you'll get booked, but you'll find that these will often be unpaid or low-pay opportunities.

3. Get Intentional

Do your research and shortlist the stages you'd love to speak on. Not all speaking opportunities are of equal calibre. Approaching a handful of high-quality events each year will have a great impact on your business and bottom line rather than an untargeted approach.

4. Understand the Market

Take the time to understand the speaking market. This will allow you to make better decisions and position yourself best for speaking opportunities. In the same way that not understanding the PR industry can mean that you struggle to get picked up by a publication, not understanding the speaking industry can lead to rookie mistakes that cost you opportunities.

When you understand the speaking industry, you know that people don't pay for your story. You appreciate that you simply can't outsource your bookings to an agent when you don't have a profile. When you know the market, you understand what a client's expectations are.

Far too many people treat their speaking as a hobby, rather than a business. And as such, they have lots of low or unpaid gigs that don't grow their business or income.

5. Optimise Your Profile

Simply having a great speaker profile isn't enough! Event organisers and speaker bookers are on a constant hunt for excellent speakers. They are busy and often won't look far beyond the first page of Google, or LinkedIn. This means that if you aren't ranking on these two search engines for your area of expertise, then you simply will not be in the running for events that you are perfect for.

An un-optimised profile is one of the main reasons great speakers don't get found. I strongly recommend beginning with optimising your LinkedIn profile. It's easy to do, requires no technical skill and you'll find a little work goes an incredibly long way. So much so, that some of my clients have increased their inbound enquires by simply taking time to learn how to optimise their profiles for niche, specific keywords.

If you want to get more publicity opportunities through speaking, where should you start?

Define what publicity means to you. More often than not, people use the words 'publicity' and 'visibility' interchangeably. If you are speaking to the wrong audiences, it doesn't build your profile or credibility with your ideal client. This means having a very clear understanding of where speaking fits into your business. Are you speaking to build your credibility, generate revenue or to build your business? Your goal will help define what a great publicity opportunity is for your business.

What about getting featured on more panels?

Event organisers book experts who speak. So, if you want more speaking opportunities on panels, or as a keynote, become a thought-leader. Demonstrate your expertise consistently. The biggest mistake that people make is focusing on becoming a great public speaker, rather than becoming a sought-after thought-leader who speaks! It's the latter that gets paid to share their expertise.

What really helps you to stand out as a public speaker?
Your expertise, the impact you have and your ability to communicate it.

Experts with a unique take get paid. Rather than being yet another XYZ speaker. Think about your unique take or a niche that will help you to stand out. We live in an information age, we can Google anything, so what am I going to get from listening to you, that I can't get from a quick Google search?

Your expertise needs depth.

Do you need to have a 'niche' as a speaker and how can you decide what that is?
It really depends on your objective. If your goal is to get paid well as a speaker, then you'll struggle to do this by being all things to all people.

Specialists get paid higher than generalists. It is possible to speak on multiple topics if there is a common thread to all your topics such that you really speak on a single theme. It's your job to clarify how all the topics you speak about go together.

If your goal is to be a well-paid speaker:

- Decide what you want to be known for.
- Research the market to understand what's in demand.
- Align your positioning to an in-demand topic or theme.
- Lead with a single topic or theme.

Becoming a highly sought-after speaker takes time and action. It means putting yourself out there, researching and consistently networking. But it positions you to share your knowledge and expertise and provide value to the world.

Lovelda Vincenzi
https://www.lovelda.com/

NETWORKING

I aim to meet ten new people professionally every month and have five 'coffee dates' with other people in my industry. This is the form of networking that works for me over formal networking events or evenings, but find what works for you and try to stick to a plan for at least three months.

Networking doesn't have to be cringey, stuffy or icky; there are lots of great in-person events that are accessible and a relaxed way to meet people. Networking is important for visibility – the more you're seen by people, the more potential connections you'll have and opportunities that will present themselves, so remember to keep those networks fresh and keep talking to people (especially when you don't need anything from them!).

PUBLIC SPEAKING

I think every founder should have a keynote talk they are ready to give at a moment's notice. Choose two or three headline topics that you could comfortably speak about when asked and position yourself as an expert on these topics – choose something that's relevant to the world today or in the news and pitch it out to event organisers and corporates.

PODCASTS

Having your own podcast is a great way to build your personal brand offline. Not only can it be good networking, when you invite other high-profile guests on, but it's a new way to touch an audience and connect with them more deeply. The podcast market is quite saturated so try to innovate around a topic. Think of a format that hasn't been done before, invite guests that haven't featured on many other podcasts, or make the podcast multi-media rich by also filming it and putting it on YouTube.

PRINT AND BROADCAST MEDIA

If you want to be visible offline as well as online, then get yourself in people's hands and ears! Print and broadcast are two great ways to do this. Focus your efforts on getting yourself into print publications and follow broadcast producers on social media for opportunities to appear on radio and TV. So much of pitching is about confidence – get confident in yourself and your expertise, and put yourself out there.

BOOKS

Speaking of getting in people's hands, writing a book is another great brand-building exercise as a founder. If you think you've got a book in you, why not write a proposal, and send it around to publishers. Lots of publishers will take a book without an agent or you can self-publish as a starting point. Non-fiction is a popular medium for business owners as it can be a strategic way to share your expertise while also building your own profile and press appeal.

WORKBOOK: YOUR VISIBILITY BLUEPRINT

There's lots of information in this chapter about how to boost your visibility as a founder, so here are some questions to help you create your own plan going forward. Let's work out how you're going to approach building your brand with clarity and focus:

1. What are your key takeaways from this chapter?

2. What platforms would you like to focus on for your own social media?

3. What goals would you like to reach with online visibility?

4. How will you measure the success of your visibility blueprint?

5. What's a sign that your plan is working?

6. Where would you like to be in six months with your visibility plan?

7. What's the big goal for your career personally over the next five years?

CHAPTER FIVE

How to Discover the Story of Your Brand

At the heart of PR is storytelling. Everything begins with a story.

Story is key to generating media attention for yourself and your brand. We need stories to build empathy, trust and relationships – they are what draw us in, make us *feel* more and connect with individuals on a deeper level.

Your chances of landing coverage, really, are about the strength and quality of your story – how unique it is, how personal, how special. Of course, how you package it is important, but at the core, the story is what matters.

We know from Simon Sinek's famous 2009 TEDx talk 'Start with why: how great leaders inspire action', and his bestselling book of the same name, that your 'why' is crucial for both your own connection to your work and how other people relate to it – why you're doing this work, what motivates and inspires you. People don't connect with what you do, but why you do it.

I would go a step further and say that 'why' should be the driving force behind your PR plan – understanding what matters about the work you're doing and what you really want people to know about it. That desire can shape and guide your plan.

For example, when I was creating a PR plan for my second book, *Unattached: Empowering Essays on Singlehood*, while the goal was to get publicity for the book, the deeper why was to help women everywhere feel a stronger sense of community around being single, feel supported and 'seen' by the book. I knew clearly how I wanted women to feel when they picked up the book and what the deeper message of the book was – that being single is something to be celebrated, not ashamed of – and that storytelling shaped my PR journey with the book. That why was real and authentic to me – it drove a lot of my press outreach, and acted as a clear hook for publications, as they understood the purpose of the book on a deeper level.

As such, I think it's important to spend time thinking about what your personal story is – the story you really want to tell – and hone your ability to seek out and tell good stories. Learning the art of storytelling will serve you in years to come; if you can discern strong stories for yourself and successfully tell them, this will be useful not only for your PR plan, but for all aspects of your business, such as marketing, copywriting and social media.

Story is the fabric that connects us more deeply with a company or brand, and if you can weave that story, you'll bring new people into your world. So, what story do you want to tell?

WHY STORY MATTERS

At the heart of every good story, there is growth – look at your personal journey and ask what's unique within that. Often conflict or struggle is what makes things interesting – you may have overcome a particular hurdle or setback, had a personal experience that caused a sudden and drastic change in your life or career.

These are the stories that are interesting and noteworthy to journalists – the ones of overcoming adversity, challenging the status quo, or achieving something against the odds. Drawing on personal experiences as much as possible is useful; this will help give your story richness and depth, and distinctiveness that other people can't offer.

Numbers and stats only tell one version of a story – and can feel a bit impersonal. Going on a deeper level to look at some of the driving factors behind a business, a passion or a desire roots it more deeply in the world and helps journalists connect with your work.

When pitching, you want to create an emotional connection with an editor as quickly as possible – this means bringing the human element to the fore in your pitch in order to catch their eye. What makes your pitch stand out next to another is your ability to make it uniquely and unapologetically your own.

You might not actually realise what the most interesting thing about your business is until you start to do this work on storytelling, so don't be tempted to rush into your PR plan before considering what your deeper story is.

WHAT MAKES A GOOD PR STORY?

There are some building blocks of a great PR story which are important for you to consider within your PR plan. I've broken these down below to make things easy for you.

1. **Know your brand story** – as we'll explore in this chapter, having a compelling brand story is a great foundation for pitches. This story needs to have a strong hook, be succinct and incorporate key elements of your brand without feeling *too* obviously branded.

2. **Make it personal** – personal is powerful. A good PR story is one that captivates audiences and is something only you can tell.

3. **Keep it simple** – a common mistake in creating a PR story is overcomplication. A good PR story shouldn't be filled with jargon, technical language or complicated phrases. And don't give everything away in the pitch. Keep it simple and under three paragraphs if you can.

4. **Write well or hire a professional writer** – I cannot stress the importance of a story being well written. If you have the budget, hire a professional writer to craft your story in the best possible language.

5. **Think about your call to action** – story is one part of the puzzle, but what's the purpose of your story? This is useful to

think about – is there a particular call to action for readers and a deeper purpose to sharing your story? Take some time to consider the intention of your story and its context in your wider PR plan.

MY PR SUCCESS STORY:
AARON WALLACE

Name: Aaron Wallace
Age: 33
Job title: Founder of Aaron Wallace

Tell me about your brand?
Aaron Wallace is the UK's first Black-owned grooming brand for Black men, founded by South London barber Aaron Wallace and his business partner, Lina Barker. They are dedicated to inspiring Black men to be the best they can be with natural hair, beard and skincare products that contain only the best natural ingredients. We use ingredients including mango butter and black seed oil, which are both rich and full of antioxidants that replenish moisture without stripping away the natural oils. Our products are all about balance and helping Black men develop a healthy hair routine. Not only do we want to enrich and strengthen Black hair; we want to instil confidence and let Black men know they've got a product they can turn to.

What's the 'why' of your business?
The male grooming sector suffers massively from a lack of diversity, and we are determined to change that by creating products that address the very specific needs of a group of people who are completely ignored in that respect.

What's your PR success story?
In 2020 we had the pleasure of securing a feature with *Forbes*.

The journalist at the time was using his platform to raise the profile of Black and under-represented entrepreneurs, who are often overlooked. After an exchange via Twitter DMs he expressed an interest in our story and wanted to write about us for *Forbes*. This was a complete game-changer. As soon as the article was published, we immediately saw the impact on our sales. The traffic to our website increased overnight, our Instagram following went up and, best of all, it led to features in *GQ, AskMen, Metro* and many more. This was just the beginning of the impact this feature would have on our business.

What have been some of the benefits of publicity for your business?

Publicity like that puts you in front of certain people and can open doors much faster than they would otherwise. What started with a Twitter DM, led to the *Forbes* article and ultimately led to us launching our natural afro hair products with giants like ASOS, Liberty London, Saks Fifth Avenue, Debenhams, Zalando and, most recently, nationwide with one of Britain's leading supermarkets, Sainsbury's. As a small Black-owned business with such a niche focus, the idea that we could one day be stocked by mainstream retailers felt unrealistic. We had the intention to focus solely on our direct-to-consumer channel as we knew this was our best chance for success. Of course, we had hopes of one day in the distant future ending up on shelves but had the feeling that this was unlikely to happen. Our feature in *Forbes* changed that and opened those doors for us much faster than we could have anticipated. We strongly believe that it was that article that gave our brand visibility and, more importantly, credibility.

Aaron Wallace
https://byaaronwallace.com/

STORY: ALL ABOUT THE DIFFERENTIATION

While there's no hard and fast rule about what makes a great story, a good starting point is thinking about what you can offer a publication that perhaps no one else can.

Think about something you can exclusively offer and what's unique to you.

PR is about differentiation, what sets you apart from the rest. Put the time in to consider those points of differentiation – this is beneficial as a business practice as a whole, and will boost your confidence with pitching.

Here are some questions to consider as a starting point for crafting a great story:

⇨ Exclusive access – do you have access that no one else does? Are you the best person to write this story? If so, why?

⇨ Are you passionate about this topic? Do you think it's unique and yet to be covered?

⇨ Is this story relevant to the publication? Does it fit with their demographic, target audience, content style and politics? Do your research first.

FINDING INSPIRATION FOR STORIES

Good stories are happening all around us, but first we must learn to listen.

The more you listen and notice the conversations happening around you – whether that's at work, in your business, in the pub, at events – the better placed you are to pitch something that feels relevant to the world right now.

I think storytelling, in essence, starts with active listening, and everything else flows from there.

Stuck on what to pitch? Here's some inspiration to unearth great stories:

⇨ What conversations have you heard around you recently? What problems are people facing right now?

⇨ Is there someone inspiring within your organisation that would make a great interview?

⇨ Have you seen a trend emerging that hasn't been covered extensively?

⇨ Do you think you've stumbled on the next big thing?

⇨ Do you have information or insights through your work that others don't?

⇨ Are you passionate about a topic or have a unique personal story?

STORIES

Stories are everywhere – you just need to know where to look. Start by noticing the conversations happening around you and how they could be used to inspire storytelling around your business.

TRENDS

Trends are another interesting line of enquiry for PR pitching. If you can spot a trend and find a relevant way to link your business or work into this trend, that's very attractive to journalists. We must remember that all stories, even in the lifestyle or wellness space, should link back to news in some capacity. Trendspotting is a good way to create that connection and keep things newsworthy.

ACCESS

Access is another fascinating avenue to explore; if you've got access to something that others may not, that automatically sets you apart. I think that's often why there's such a focus on 'exclusives' in journalism – we want to feel that the story we're receiving is somehow special to us, and if you're providing access to a story that hasn't been covered before, that provides a level of exclusivity and intrigue. Every journalist wants to be the first on a story, and the more high-level access you're able to provide, the more appealing the story.

PROBLEM-SOLVING

I mention problems here also, because I think if your business, product or service solves people's pain points in a genuine way, that's very interesting to a journalist. At the end of the day, they're trying to help, support and inform their readers through features – and being able to relate to them and show how a business is changing the world for the better or solving a problem through their work always makes a good story. For me, a compelling story is one that's informative and helpful in some capacity – and you can trace most good stories back to this desire to be of service to readers.

If you feel comfortable sharing your personal story, this can be a great starting point for pitching – no one is going to have the same story as you. Drawing on your uniqueness is a great starting point. Below are some ideas to dig a little deeper into that personal story and build layers of intrigue that make it compelling and real.

EXERCISE:
PROMPTS FOR DISCOVERING YOUR PERSONAL STORY

Stuck on what to pitch? Here are some prompts to think about for your work that may inspire stories of your own – grab a pen and paper and get brainstorming:

⇨ What are you doing to make the world a better place?
⇨ What's the inspiration or motivation behind the work you do?
⇨ What's your why?
⇨ What's special about your personal experience and journey?
⇨ What challenges have you overcome to make your business a success?
⇨ Do you have a special niche?
⇨ How do you stand out from others in your industry?
⇨ How are you doing things differently?

STORY TIPS: WHAT EDITORS WANT

Again, while there's no one rule for what makes a good story to an editor, I would say there are a few verticals within publications that are always popular and editors are often looking for, which you might like to pitch in for. I've included these below, along with some tips for each to help your pitch stand out:

⇨ First-person and opinion pieces
⇨ Human interest stories
⇨ How-to and top tips articles
⇨ Money and finance features
⇨ Taboo-breaking features
⇨ Career change features
⇨ Interesting takes on failure and business lessons
⇨ Interview features

FIRST-PERSON AND OPINION PIECES

Editors like opinions. If you have them, share them.

Don't be afraid of shooting your shot. Most publications have an 'Opinions' or 'Views' section, and this can be a great place to position yourself as a thought-leader. That's why I press the importance of developing your writing skills – I think it can be very beneficial for business owners to pitch themselves to write personally and advance that side of their personal brand.

Of course, there are potential risks of sharing opinions publicly and you must be emotionally prepared for backlash, as it can happen. So make sure you feel strongly about your case and are ready to defend your corner if needs be – and you're not saying something you'll regret in years to come.

HUMAN INTEREST STORIES

With human interest stories, we tend to think of magazines like *Take a Break* that might be read in the hairdresser's, which are sensationalist and a touch vulgar. But there's definitely a classy way of doing human interest stories and they can be a compelling way to share your PR story.

My advice if you're pitching a human-interest story is not to make it too over the top – I tend to see a lot of hyperbolism being used with these kinds of stories, overuse of adjectives and a sense of drama. In fact, human interest stories can be more subtle and nuanced, it's just about how you tell them.

You don't need to tell a sob story for the sake of it and if you're not comfortable with this kind of storytelling, don't force it. But if you do have a compelling human-interest story to tell, don't be afraid of being vulnerable; as Brené Brown says, vulnerability is what connects us to others, it's a 'thickener' between individuals and can create a ripple effect of compassion and understanding from others.

HOW-TO AND TOP TIPS ARTICLES

Another good starting point for stories is thinking about what practical know-how you've developed through your work and how this could be applied editorially. How-to and tips-based articles are always popular on websites and are something editors are often looking to run more of.

Always check they haven't been run before – again, you want to think about something special and different that you could give advice on. Have a brainstorm of what practical insights or expertise you could lend to a publication and use this as inspiration for pitching.

MONEY AND FINANCE FEATURES

Money and personal finance used to be quite taboo topics, but they've become huge in the mainstream in the last few years, especially during the pandemic when so many people found their work and financial situation changing drastically. I think the after-effect of that is we're much more open talking about money and wanting to share personal experiences around money.

Money-based conversations are an interesting angle to explore – this might be around raising finance for a business, getting out of debt, turning things around financially or tips for how to generate more revenue. Business publications such as *Business Insider* and *Forbes* often commission writers to cover finance and if you've got good insights on anything in the money arena, you'll be well placed to be covered in these kinds of publications.

TABOO-BREAKING FEATURES

Are there conversations that you don't feel we're having which we should be? Follow that instinct.

Work on a story that raises awareness around a topic or breaks a taboo – again, this is coming back to the idea that the role of publications is to inform, surprise and delight their audience. It can be beneficial to back up this kind of feature with statistics or research to give it legitimacy and make it stand out to editors. You don't ever want to be inventing a trend or a taboo that's not actually there, so whatever you can do to back up your idea with evidence is great.

CAREER CHANGE FEATURES

Personally, I'm always interested to hear about when someone has made a big change in their career. These stories can be very inspiring to read and people love hearing about what's possible when we decide to make a change for ourselves, and the circumstances that inspire that change. It's a reminder that anything is possible and our timelines are never linear.

If you've made a drastic change, you could use this as inspiration for pitching a great story – it could be personal, for example what you learnt from that change, or be advice-led, sharing how other people could do the same.

BUSINESS LESSONS

Perhaps because of the pandemic, I've noticed a rise in features around failure and interesting takes on what failure means, and what we can learn from it. Success stories are not always the most interesting ones; and I think success after failure is much richer to read. Think about your personal story and if there's been some angle on failure you could explore.

Beyond that, business lessons are evergreen and are popular on most websites – these often take the form of lists, such as '7 things I learnt from exiting my company'. Listicles of this kind are often like soundbites; we want things that are punchy, easy to digest and shareable. You want to get straight to the point and draw inspiration from your personal journey to offer something truly insightful.

INTERVIEW FEATURES

Almost every website and newspaper will have an interview section of some kind – and these are some of the most coveted spots in a publication, and the hardest to pitch into. I'm pitched dozens of interviewees every day and it can be hard to stand out in these kinds of features, as there are always more great candidates for interview than spaces in a paper or website.

If you're pitching yourself or someone else to be interviewed, I would say remember to do your homework. Check the kind of people they normally cover in the publication and try to work out why that person is noteworthy to the publication – there may be credentials or expertise that they value – and you need to make sure the individual is a good fit for the publication.

Other brand assets are valuable here too. Being able to offer great photography or video content is a real plus with interview pitches. You want to have great photography (both portrait and landscape) that shows the individuals in the best, most professional light. Also, considering offering an interview as an exclusive can be another thing that's beneficial to support your pitch and its chances of landing.

CASE STUDY:
ALI PANTONY ON HOW TO GET FEATURED
IN GLAMOUR UK

Ali Pantony is acting website director of Glamour UK, covering everything from lifestyle, wellness and mental health to beauty, empowerment and activism. Here are her top tips on getting featured in Glamour magazine:

Name: Ali Pantony
Age: 30
Job title: Acting website director, Glamour UK

What are some top tips you can share on PR working with journalists?

Get to know the publication you're pitching to. It sounds basic, but I receive an awful lot of irrelevant pitches. For example, at Glamour, we work hard to challenge the toxic and unrealistic beauty standards forced on women. So, if you pitch me a story on 'how to shift the Christmas pounds', it's not going to fly. Read the publication you want to be featured in every day. What are their core content pillars? What's at the top of their homepage and what are their website's channels and tags? What are their readers interested in? What is their audience passionate about? Then tailor your pitch and press release accordingly.

When someone gets in touch with a story, what makes you take notice?

Firstly, your subject line is so important. I get hundreds of emails every day, and if I'm being totally honest here, half of them don't even get opened (if I read every email, I wouldn't have time to do my actual job). I can tell from your subject line whether the email is going to be useful to me and my publication. Keep it snappy, and leave out the fluff. Think: what would the headline be if this were turned into an article? Then keep the email concise (a couple of paragraphs will do) with relevant links and images in the body of the email.

Make sure it's a story we haven't run before (top tip: type 'site:*glamourmagazine.co.uk* + KEYWORD' into Google to see if we've already covered what you're pitching). Glamour's a beauty-first, industry-leading brand, so if you're pitching me 'how to look after dry skin', I'm going to hit delete – it's well-trodden ground for us. What makes your story new, fresh and newsworthy? Why now, and why Glamour? Make it extra juicy with relevant figures, stats and case studies, and now we're talking.

What really turns you off as a journalist?

- PRs who have very little understanding of our brand and what we stand for.
- Sending irrelevant information.
- Chasing too soon and too often. Journalists will respond to your initial email if it is of interest.
- Asking me to send links or, when I was on print, cuttings. Support the brand you're trying to be featured in by giving us the clicks or going to a shop and buying our magazine.
- WeTransfers. That. Expire. In. 7. Days.
- Not including images for or links to the product you're trying to get featured.
- Demanding OTT branding in editorial – not advertorial – coverage.

What makes a good story in your eyes?

Something I haven't read before. Good storytelling is about taking something topical and newsworthy and making it interesting and valuable to your audience. It'll have a hook – the reason you're telling the story – then the angle that makes it relevant to our publication, showing what our readers are going to take away from it. When we're discussing the morning news at Glamour, the most common question we ask is: 'What's the

Glamour angle here?' – what makes our take on this story different to everyone else's. If we can't answer that question, it's probably not the story for us.

But perhaps most importantly, good storytelling comes when a writer cares deeply about what they're writing. As an editor – and a reader – you can tell when the story really means something to them. My team's best pieces of writing have been about stories they're passionate about. Be raw, be honest and delve deep into the subject. Leave no stone unturned. That's what makes a story stick with you long after you've finished reading.

Ali Pantony
Follow her on Twitter @alipantony

WORKBOOK: DISCOVERING THE STORY OF YOUR BRAND

It's time to get scribbling. Take some time to consider what you've learnt from this chapter and how you can apply these lessons to inspire storytelling within business:

1. What did you learn about storytelling in this chapter?

2. How confident do you feel about crafting stories now?

3. What areas of your business do you think will generate the most interesting stories?

4. How personal are you willing for your story pitches to be?

5. What types of articles would work best for your pitches?

6. What personal story are you keen to tell about yourself?

CHAPTER SIX

How to Build Your Media Network

In this chapter, we'll be looking at how to find media outlets and build a network of journalist contacts you can incorporate into your PR strategy. It goes without saying that without contacts your PR plan has nowhere to go.

We'll also be looking at how you build rapport with journalists and what you can do to build good PR relations. It's one thing to find the right contact, it's another to form a genuine relationship with them.

I'll be sharing everything about how journalists like to work and how to build a relationship that is reciprocal and mutually beneficial.

The cornerstone of any PR strategy is having your own personal database of journalists' contact details. You need to send your pitch to the right journalists if you want to succeed with earned media – and people often find it difficult to locate the right people.

As a starting point, I have some tips on how to choose the best person to pitch at a publication, as it's not as straightforward as you might think.

GUIDE: CONTACTING THE RIGHT JOURNALISTS

Very often, we want to go to the top person at a publication to send a story, as we think they have the most authority there. But, in fact, going to the editor-in-chief is not always the best idea – they are the most senior at a publication, and will often not be involved in the day-to-day production of stories, but instead be managing teams and overseeing the publication overall. You don't want someone who is looking after the overarching direction of the publication, but the staff writer in charge of writing articles.

So, instead, you must be a bit tactical about who you approach with your story. Here are some insights into different job roles at publications and what their day-to-day position might involve:

EDITOR-IN-CHIEF

An editor-in-chief is the main manager of any print or digital publication, which could be a physical newspaper, online magazine and/or website. They will oversee the publication as a whole, deciding the look and feel of the brand's editorial output. They will have the final word on any big editorial decisions, and will manage and lead the team of editors, copyeditors and writers that make up the publication's editorial team.

FEATURES EDITOR

Features editors are one rung beneath the editor-in-chief at a publication. They are also sometimes referred to as the commissioning editor or managing editor and their job may involve commissioning freelance writers for the publication, writing and editing. A features editor role includes assigning articles to writers, reading pitches from freelancers, commissioning, and maintaining the publication's 'house style' through a clear editorial voice and vision. A features editor will also write and research articles for the website and edit content from other writers.

SECTION EDITOR

A section editor, such as a fashion editor, health editor or news editor, will normally report to the features editor. A section editor's role is specific to their area of expertise, but the day-to-day responsibilities will include managing the production of articles, writing, researching and working with freelance writers. These specific editors are often the best ones to contact for press events.

STAFF WRITER

Most publications will have staff writers who are responsible for most of the writing output. Staff writers work across sections and will be interested in hearing about ideas for different verticals. This job is more junior (sometimes they are called junior writers) and may involve travelling for a story, especially in news, where the role involves a lot of on-the-ground reporting.

FEATURES INTERN

Many publications will also have features interns, who pick up some of the writing work. An intern can be expected to work across different sections of the publication, assist on social media and work with the editorial team to bring features to life.

Top tip: I would always endeavour to make your pitch as relevant as possible, so would recommend contacting a section editor who has written extensively about the topic you're pitching. Do your homework to make sure they have covered this topic before and it would be interesting to them.

SEVEN WAYS TO FIND JOURNALIST CONTACT DETAILS

There's no magic trick to finding the right contact at a publication, but it's not a total mystery either. PR agencies will have you believe that you need a 'little black book' of contacts to get media coverage, but this of course serves their own agenda. The truth is you're totally able to do the work yourself and build your own contacts; you just need to get a little creative about things.

The first step is to be clear about who you want to contact and why. I would always advise to be strategic and only try reaching out to a small number of publications at any one time. You don't want to take a blanket approach; instead, you want to narrow down the key publications for you and be more tailored in your outreach.

Here are some ways to find contacts at different publications:

1. PAY FOR A MEDIA DATABASE

The simplest way to get contact details for journalists is using a paid-for media database. If you don't have budget for this, there are lots of other ways of going about it, but this is by far the most time efficient. In the UK, these are the databases that are best for securing media contacts:

⇨ **Roxhill Media** – Probably the best media database in the UK. You can discover the journalists who are most interested in your chosen topic and search by topic, sector, keyword and company to create a target list of ideal journalists for your pitch.

⇨ **Gorkana** – This is the UK's leader in media intelligence. They offer media analysis, a media database, media monitoring and social media tracking.

⇨ **ResponseSource** – As a paid member of ResponseSource, you'll have access to the Vuelio Media Database, which provides media data, alongside monitoring, analysis and reporting, designed to save you time.

⇨ **Cision** – Cision offers PR and marketing solutions to get you in the right inbox quicker. Their media relationship management tool comes with a vetted global database of over 1.1 billion influencers. This can help you streamline your outreach and pitch the right journalist instantly.

⇨ **Agility PR** – This software can help you with your entire outreach strategy. You can find journalists and influencers who will be interested in your story, save and update lists, send pitches and press releases and track the success of your PR plan.

⇨ **Muck Rack** – This is a user-friendly media database, which is intuitive and easy to use.

Note: these databases will vary in their price and usage, but most offer free trials and will often give discounted rates to start-ups, so it's always worth asking.

2. START WITH TWITTER

Twitter can be a very helpful tool for finding relevant journalists for your pitch and building relationships. It's probably the best social platform for media relations – here's how to do it:

⇨ **Start searching** – the best way to find journalists is by searching for writers at a publication.

⇨ **Find the right people** – start by looking up the titles, for example *Harper's Bazaar*, and then filter by 'People' at the top, which should refine the search to journalists that have that publication in their bio.

⇨ **Do your research** – it may be helpful to look for journalists who are verified on Twitter, as they are often the current journalists at an outlet.

⇨ **Get organised** – it may also be helpful to create a 'List' on Twitter of relevant journalists once you've found them – this means you'll have all contacts in one place. You can refer to these lists when crafting a pitch and find relevant contacts for your story.

⇨ **Perfect your profile** – if you're going to be using Twitter regularly, then make sure your bio is up to speed. If not, it's time to optimise it. You want to make your industry and work clear. Make sure you have a professional profile photo.

GOLDEN RULES:
HOW TO USE TWITTER TO BUILD RELATIONSHIPS WITH JOURNALISTS

Want to use Twitter more strategically? Here are some golden rules for Twitter by The Two Lauras, social media marketing psychology experts and founders of The Hub for Social Media Managers Ltd:

1. Before even considering connecting with journalists on Twitter it's important to optimise your profile. This means ensuring your Twitter bio tells people what you want to be known for, and it should include a link to your website. Your most recent content and pinned post must be relevant to whatever it is you want to be known for.

You should do this for all of your social media platforms so you know you are prepared for anyone visiting your profile as a result of media coverage.

2. Next, you need to find the journalists you wish to build a relationship with on Twitter. Many journalists use #JournoRequest when they are looking for help, so take a look at the feed and check out the profiles of any journalists who have recently tweeted a request, even if what they are looking for right now isn't relevant to you. When you visit their profile be sure to look at their content and find out who they write for and what they write about. By discovering their style of writing you'll start to understand whether you might be right for their future articles and will learn how best to spin your story to meet their needs.

3. Build an authentic relationship. We hear the word 'authentic' thrown around a lot on social media but it's really important to act like a normal human on Twitter in order to build a relationship.

To do this, start natural conversations with the journalists you want to engage with. Read and let them know how much you've enjoyed their latest articles – be honest, don't tell them you've enjoyed something if you've not even read it!

If your followers would also enjoy their articles, quote tweet it so they can read it too. This is a brilliant way of not only building a relationship with the journalist, but also providing valuable content for your audience.

But don't be lazy and simply retweet it, instead use the quote tweet function to give your followers a reason to read the article by telling them what you enjoyed and what's in it for them.

Authentic relationships are often built by being helpful, and that is true of Twitter too. You can be helpful on Twitter by sharing a journalist's PR request and tagging someone who you know might be suitable to help them with their article.

As humans we all remember the people who have helped us in the past so try not to only respond to their tweets when their request is something you want to help with directly.

4. Turn on notifications. Twitter is a busy place and journalists will often be looking for a quick turnaround, so once you discover journalists who you think might align with your goals for PR, be sure to turn on notifications so you don't miss any of their tweets. Check in regularly to build a relationship with them.

5. Use social listening tools such as Agorapulse to get notified of certain keywords so you can respond to requests specifically about your area of expertise, industry, niche or product.

6. Set up Twitter lists of your favourite journalists so you can quickly scroll through a feed of their content, avoiding distraction and saving time in the main busy Twitter feed. Be careful how you name your Twitter list as anyone being added to a public list will be notified.

You could also consider using TweetDeck to display multiple feeds on your desktop rather than switching between lists throughout the day.

7. Remember the golden rule of engaging on Twitter: add value. Don't distract someone with a notification that they have a comment only for them to log in and see it's a simple heart emoji! If you're going to take the time to respond to someone, make sure it's worthwhile.

8. The best way to respond to journo requests is to do whatever the journalist asks of you. They're busy people so if you spot a request on Twitter, be sure to read it properly and only DM if they ask you to. Often they'll direct you to email them so check their bio for the email address before asking for it.

The Two Lauras
https://thetwolauras.com/

3. MAKE THE MOST OF LINKEDIN

LinkedIn is another good platform for finding journalists' contact details. Here's how to use LinkedIn to your advantage:

⇨ **Study their profile** – Before you make a connection request, make sure you've done your homework and looked at their profile. Look at the publications they have worked at before and if they have any special interest subject matters.

⇨ **Connect personally** – If you're going to add journalists on LinkedIn, you want to make it personal, as it can feel quite spammy as a platform with people asking to connect when you don't know each other. So, make it relevant to the journalist, include a personal note when adding them and perhaps explain why you think you'd be a great connection or how you can be of value to them.

⇨ **Use LinkedIn to find their details** – Many journalists will have their contact details listed on their profile, which can be handy if you're building a journalist database. They will often also have their other social media handles listed there, and I'd always recommend following them on other social channels as well.

⇨ **Be part of the action** – There are lots of great groups on LinkedIn that journalists may be part of, so do your research to find relevant groups that may offer up press opportunities. This is handy as you can message other members of the group even if you're not connected, which is a good way of staying in touch without being pushy.

⇨ **Follow the publications** – Another good idea is to follow the publications on LinkedIn so you can stay informed with the most recent articles. You may also hear about new hires, which is useful for keeping tabs on relevant journalists.

⇨ **Make yourself searchable** – It's also important to think about your own profile and how it will be received by journalists. Make sure that your profile will appear in searches – your profile is seven times more likely to be viewed if you add a photo and twelve times more likely if you add more than one position. Choose a keyword that you'd like to rank for and make sure this is well used throughout your profile to give yourself more chance of showing up in searches.

⇨ **Engage more** – The more you engage on LinkedIn, the more interaction you'll get on your profile. So dedicate time every day to actually engage with the platform, sharing stories from journalists and commenting. This is a good way to generate warm leads for when you actually do pitch.

HOW TO USE LINKEDIN TO GROW YOUR NETWORK – AND YOUR BUSINESS

Want to grow your reach on LinkedIn? Here are some top tips from Phil Szomszor, partner at Brightside Digital Engagement:

I left agency life at the end of 2019, having been an employee for over twenty years. My wife and I were starting a new venture and each announced what we were doing on LinkedIn.

Forty-eight hours later, I got a message from an ex-client called Julian, who I first worked with in 2005.

'Hi, Phil, I've seen you've set up a marketing consultancy. I think I need your help.'

A couple of days later, we'd signed one of our first major clients.

That's the power of LinkedIn and I see it every day. What

are the chances that I would have got in touch with Julian, having not spoken in such a long time?

In the last couple of years, LinkedIn has really taken off.

The pandemic meant that people suddenly couldn't meet face to face for sales meetings or pitches, so LinkedIn filled the void. During that period content creation went up 60 per cent and conversations increased 55 per cent.[1]

And it hasn't just been a pandemic fad – membership and usage of LinkedIn has continued to rise.

The question is, how can you leverage it to grow your business?

Four Steps to LinkedIn Success

1. Look the part

Set up your profile and consider it in terms of an elevator pitch, rather than a CV. So, in your bio (the About section), talk about the problem you solve, rather than your work history and enjoyment of the theatre.

Quick tip: Make sure you get a good quality profile picture that clearly shows your face. Essentially, this is your personal logo.

2. Get connected

Think of LinkedIn as your personal customer database. If you haven't already done so, go back through your work history and make connections with everyone who could help you – ex-customers and clients, journalists, colleagues, bosses ... You never know where the opportunities could come from.

Quick tip: Always write a 'note' when you send an invitation to give context to the connection request.

3. Engage in conversations

LinkedIn's algorithm rewards conversations, so make sure you

---

[1] https://www.searchenginejournal.com/linkedin-content-creation-is-up-60-compared-to-last-year/373193/

comment regularly and be generous with your knowledge and expertise. You can do this reactively, to people who have commented on your posts, or proactively on other people's posts. And don't limit this to people you are already connected with, but potential customers and influencers too.

Quick tip: Remember to tag people in the comments (using the @ symbol before typing their name), so they get a notification and will be likely to respond.

4. Publish your own content

LinkedIn has lots of content formats, but the easiest to get to grips with is a simple post. You have three thousand characters to play with, so you can do all sorts of things with them. The best posts are storytelling in nature and address audience problems or things they care about.

Quick tip: Don't overthink it, just start by writing about what you know.

Final point. Like most things in life, LinkedIn is a long game and the more you do it, the better you'll get.

Phil Szomszor
https://www.linkedin.com/in/philszomszor/

4. USE GOOGLE NEWS

Google News is a good way to find the right publications for your niche. A savvy way of doing this is to search for the names of your competitors' businesses or individuals within your industry within Google News and see where they have been featured.

Through Google News you'll get a list of publications, blogs, news sites and online magazines that they have been featured in, and this can be a helpful way of creating a database for pitching of your own. Take note of the names of the editors or journalists who have written these features, so you can pitch them in the future.

5. DON'T FORGET GOOGLE KEYWORD

Stay in the loop with current news and trends by setting up a Google Keyword alert. You can receive daily alerts through this with relevant news from your industry – this is a great way to get to know the journalists who are writing about your niche. From there, I'd then follow them on social media and keep a spreadsheet of the right people to contact. It's a good habit to do a daily scan of Google News and where these keywords have been featured.

6. EMAIL FINDER TOOLS

There are plenty of tools that will help you find email addresses for free, although it may involve some trial and error. Hunter is the leading solution for finding email addresses – and the most reliable one in the UK.

7. CHECK THE PUBLICATIONS

A basic point, but one lots of people forget – often publications will have the journalist's contact details listed on their website, so check the masthead first before doing all the other research to get contact details. I would avoid pitching any generic email address as these tend to be unmanned inboxes.

MY STRATEGY: HOW TO COURT A JOURNALIST

For the last ten years, I've built a personal strategy for building relationships with editors for my own freelance writing career. The same strategy can be applied to creating relationships with journalists that you may like to pitch your story within a PR plan.

Of course, the pandemic has changed things a lot. More writers are working remotely, teams are stretched and getting a journalist's attention is probably harder than ever. That said, I think people are keen to refresh their networks post-pandemic and there's never a bad time to get in touch with journalists, it's just being savvy about how you use their time and what you're asking for.

TRY TO GET FACE TO FACE

I believe the best way to build a relationship with a journalist is to get face to face with them. Always.

It's so much easier and better to build a connection in real life, and I think after so many months of isolation during the pandemic, we have more of a desire for in-person connection.

I would always try to invite a journalist out for coffee and speak in person – this is going to be easier if you work for a PR agency, as you will represent multiple clients, and it's in a journalist's best interest to build a relationship with you. But, even as a business owner, with the right approach you should be able to set up an in-person meeting, or even a quick coffee virtually.

One piece of advice I can share here is to be complimentary in an introductory email – tell them you really like their work, share thoughts on a recent article they have written or respond to something they've recently posted on social media. You want to keep it 'warm' and not feel like you're selling them something too early on – for that reason, I think compliments are very important.

Something like:

Dear X

I really loved that article you wrote on women and NFTs for Grazia – it's such an interesting space and I think the conversation around how to get women more involved in investing is so important.

With that in mind, I was wondering if I could invite you out for a quick coffee to tell you a bit more about my financial advice platform and how we could collaborate editorially together in the future.

Alternatively, I'd be happy to tell you a bit more over a coffee on Zoom.

Let me know if there's a time in the next week that works for you to grab twenty-five minutes of your time to talk.

Best,

X

INVITE THEM TO SOMETHING THEY REALLY WANT TO DO

Another piece of advice here is to invite them to something they *really* want to do. We often fall into the same habits – going for an early morning meeting over coffee. But I think it pays to be creative sometimes, and I've had a lot more luck meeting with editors over the years by inviting them to something they really want to do, or by making it as easy as possible for them.

Some examples of things you could invite a journalist to do with you, that doesn't involve sitting over coffee, such as:

⇨ Go to a gym class
⇨ Get a manicure
⇨ Get a blow-dry
⇨ After-work drinks

You can make it tailored and specific. Perhaps they are a whisky lover, and you could invite them to meet you over a whisky cocktail. Perhaps they love the gym and you could take them out for a spin class. Perhaps they have a dog and you could suggest a quick dog walk in the park.

Maybe it sounds trivial, but these are how relationships are built. I've built some of my best contacts in the industry by thinking outside the box and being creative with the ways that I manage to get face to face. I'll often say yes to meeting a PR agency if I'm getting a manicure out of it – and there's nothing to do but listen when your hands are occupied!

If you are struggling to get a face-to-face meeting with a journalist, another idea is to book an event that they are speaking at. Lots of publications put on their own events which are often moderated by journalists from the publication – get there early, perhaps you could help set up and build favour that way. You'll often have opportunities to network afterwards or ask questions in the Q & A part of the evening – this is a great way to generate warm leads for pitching post-event.

REMEMBER TO MAKE IT EASY FOR THEM

Most meetings are pointless, let's be honest about that. Ninety per cent of the time they are a waste of time and things can be summed up in an email.

My exception to this is when you're meeting with someone that could become a useful contact in the future and you don't want to rely on a lot of cold pitching. But most people find meetings a drag and unless there's a clear outcome to them, they probably won't say yes.

Which is why I think it's important to make meeting up as easy as possible for an editor. I would always suggest meeting up somewhere that's close to their office or where they live (depending on whether they are working at home or not). And I'd be mindful of the time you're suggesting – if they are freelance, they are rarely going to want to meet before 10 a.m. (that's the whole point of being freelance, that you don't have to be up at the crack of dawn). For example, if I was trying to meet with someone from the *Daily Mail*, whose offices are in Kensington, I would say something like 'I'd love to grab twenty minutes of your time, at the Ivy Cafe on Kensington High Street.'

The time limit is important. I'd always recommend spelling out exactly how long a meeting is going to take. Editors are busy and they want to know that they're not going to be stuck for hours talking; it's a respectful thing to do, showing that you know their time is precious and you're not going to waste it.

So make it easy for them and be clear how long an in-person conversation is going to take.

HOW TO ACT DURING AN IN-PERSON MEETING

If you do manage to get face to face, how you act at an in-person meeting with a journalist is very important. I've had many meetings where I've come away thinking, *Well, that was a waste of time*, and it's put me off working with them in future.

So, while getting a first meeting is a win, knowing how to behave on that first meeting is equally important. You need to remember it's work, and while it's good to build rapport on personal topics, try to keep it professional and explain the ways that you're able to support them in the future when working on stories.

My main advice is to remember to listen. If things go to plan, you're going to be spending the rest of your working relationship speaking *at* them: pitching ideas, selling stories, sending press releases. This is one of the very few opportunities you'll get to *listen*, to discover their working habits, to learn about how they like to work and what they do and don't want in a pitch.

So, ask questions and listen closely. This will only benefit you in the long run when you are pitching in the future.

Take a notebook with you and try to ask as many of these questions as possible:

⇨ How far ahead do you work on a story?
⇨ What kind of information are you interested in receiving? News, interview ideas, invites, press trips?
⇨ What's the most popular content in the newspaper/magazine at the moment?
⇨ What format do you like to receive information in? Press releases, PDF, Word documents?
⇨ How do you like to receive images?
⇨ What's the best way to get in touch? Do you want to be pitched on email or are phone calls better?
⇨ Are you working on any stories you need support on?
⇨ Are you open to new story ideas or do you just want support on things you're already working on?
⇨ When's the best time of the week/day to pitch ideas?

These are the questions you really want to be asking a journalist. Basically, don't make it too fluffy; you want to get a very clear idea of what works for them and what doesn't. This will be your secret weapon when it comes to pitching in the future.

MAKE A MASTER SPREADSHEET

I would then create a spreadsheet that's going to act as a masterplan for pitching in the future. List all the journalists you've met or connected with and create a reminder for yourself of how best to pitch them – this is something you can keep referring to in the future and updated as your network grows. It will basically be going to help you act a one-person PR agency, where you can create your own little black book of contacts that will prove very useful to you in the future.

I would include all the information you have – how quickly they turnaround stories, the format they like to be sent information and images in, any notes on how best to contact them. Build it and you'll give yourself a huge advantage when it comes to pitching effectively.

TOP TIPS:
CREATING RAPPORT WITH JOURNALISTS

Want to create even more rapport with journalists? Here are some quick top tips to help you do that:

1. **Engage with their work** – like, share, comment. It won't go unnoticed, and when you do come to pitch, your name already has some positive associations with supporting their work.

2. **Be complimentary** – being kind about someone's work goes far, don't forget that.

3. **Court with free stuff** – journalists like free stuff. It's just a fact. We'll explore this more in the next chapter looking at gifting and press drops, but it's worth noting that if you have a product-based business, sending out samples is an easy way to build some rapport and relationship with a journalist.

---

4. **Be speedy** – speed is everything in journalism. If you're able to provide them with something on a quick turnaround, this will help to build some trust and connection. If you can help them out and be quick about things, then do.

5. **Do favours** – even if you can't help them directly with a story, maybe you have a contact that can. Helping a journalist out, especially last minute when they are working on something on a quick turnaround, is a great way to show yourself in a positive light. You can often find these last-minute requests on Twitter, with anything marked urgent.

6. **Don't let them down** – the easiest way to break that trust is by promising something and then not being able to deliver. Don't let them down, if you've said you can support on something, then work hard to make that happen! Especially if it involves using experts or sources for stories, as these can be hard to rearrange last minute.

PR SUCCESS STORY:
JESSICA ALDERSON, CO-FOUNDER OF SO SYNCD

Jessica Alderson is the co-founder of So Syncd, a free personality type dating app. Here she shares her story on how PR has boosted her business:

Name: Jessica Alderson
Age: 31
Job title: CEO & co-founder of So Syncd

How has PR benefited your business?
PR has been an important tool to help us build a strong brand that people trust. As a dating app, it's particularly important to build trust with people because the whole process of dating is

an emotional experience. Singles are looking for a life partner and it's a huge decision. It's important that they feel aligned with the brand of the dating app they choose. PR helped us evolve from a small, unknown dating app into a dating app that people talk about with hundreds of thousands of users. In addition, SEO is a major part of our overall strategy and having links to our website from major publications has helped drive more web traffic.

What approach has helped you secure coverage?
I spend time researching each writer before pitching to them to understand what kind of topics they write about, and this helps me to work out if there is a specific angle that would best suit them. Reading articles that different journalists have written also sparks new ideas so there is an added benefit of doing this. I also have a quick look through journalists' public social media profiles to get a feel for what they are like as a person so I can adjust the tone of the email.

I have tweaked my pitch as I've gone along. It's not always clear from the very beginning as to what works the best. Like with a lot of things in life, it's about trial and error. I tried different ways of telling our story to see which got the best response. I make sure to tell our story in a way that is clear and differentiated. We are lucky to some extent because dating and personality types are topics that people love to discuss but people love to hear the backstories of all kinds of start-ups.

When I am interviewed, I don't shy away from telling the full story. Start-ups are hard and explaining how you overcame challenges is just as interesting as sharing the story behind wins, if not more so.

Any tips for a founder doing their own PR?
Always remember that it's a numbers game. Journalists are super busy and they constantly receive pitches throughout the day. Don't be disillusioned if you don't receive any responses for

days on end. It's about reaching the right journalist at the right time with the right story. It's fine to follow up with a journalist once because they might have been busy at the time you sent your initial email, but if you don't hear back after following up, just leave it. You can always reach out again in a few months with a new angle if you think that journalist is particularly relevant.

Follow journalists in your area and who cover your space on Twitter. They will often share their recent articles and they might ask for sources occasionally too.

It's important to respond to any journalist requests quickly. They often have hard deadlines and it's not ideal if you take a long time to reply.

Are there any mistakes you could have avoided?

My first pitches were too long. There is a balance between giving enough information to make it an engaging story and appreciating that people are busy and don't have time to read a pitch that is four to five lengthy paragraphs. I usually try to keep my pitches at around three paragraphs now and I have seen a higher response rate.

What's been the most successful way to pitch journalists?

I have had most success emailing journalists directly. I tried direct messaging on Twitter for a while and I did get a few responses, but email has been a more effective medium for me on balance. It's common for journalists to share their email addresses in their Twitter bios but if not, there are a number of tools you can use to find journalists' email addresses (usually for a small subscription fee). Alternatively, you can usually guess a handful of email addresses if you know the person's name and where they work. Once I messaged someone via Instagram because I couldn't find her email address. She replied and we set up an interview but I tend to avoid reaching out to journalists on Instagram if possible.

Any insights on how a tech business can get PR coverage?
My main tip would be to have a clear, engaging and simple story. Every founder has a reason as to why they started their company and usually it's a desire to solve a problem they faced themselves. Once you have a clear narrative, don't be afraid to repeat it again and again. That is one of the best ways to build a strong brand.

It's also hugely beneficial to build relationships where possible. If a journalist regularly covers stories in your space, it benefits both parties to form a long-term relationship. I have found that one of the best ways to do this is to share other potential stories with journalists. They are always looking for the next top story and interesting sources. If you can help them to find what they are looking for, it builds trust.

Jessica Alderson
https://www.sosyncd.com/

WORKBOOK: BUILDING YOUR MEDIA NETWORK

Now you've discovered some new ways to build your own media tribe, it's time for some reflection. Here are some questions to consider after reading this chapter:

1. What kind of journalists do you want to contact as part of your PR plan?

2. How are you going to go about getting media contacts?

3. Are there any paid-for services you're going to subscribe to?

4. How are you going to approach face-to-face meetings with journalists?

5. Who are the key journalists you'd like to meet in person?

CHAPTER SEVEN

How to Take Your PR Plan Further

In this chapter, we're going to explore how you can amplify your brand, through various profile-raising activities. You may want to hold a press event, collaborate with influencers or provide journalists with a gift of your product or services. This is a step further in your PR plan, as it invites journalists or influencers into your world and gives them a tangible sense of what you're all about. There are some golden rules for these actions, however, and in this chapter, I'll be giving some guidance on how to put on a successful press event and smash an influencer partnership.

While these actions can be great to amplify a print-press campaign, you also need to be strategic here about how you're working with the press and what you're hoping to get out of it. Having a clear goal in mind of what you're trying to achieve with an event, an influencer campaign or press gifting is only going to help you. So, take a moment before launching any of these activities to get clear on the objectives for your business.

Here are some questions to consider:

⇨ What activities alongside pitching stories would help amplify your PR campaign?
⇨ What boost does your business really need right now?
⇨ What kind of events would benefit your brand or business?
⇨ Would in-person or virtual events be more beneficial?
⇨ Would working with influencers support your business goals?
⇨ Do you have products that you can send out?
⇨ Do you have a service that you can offer journalists to try?
⇨ How can you complement your email pitch with products or events?

⇨   Have your competitors done anything noteworthy that can inspire you?

⇨   Are there any other relationship-building activities with the press you could do?

PRESS EVENTS

Press events can be fantastic for your business; they are a great way to network and connect with journalists face to face and showcase what your business is all about. They also can – and should – be fun and informative.

Press events shouldn't be limited to just product-based business – even if you've got a service-based offering, you can still put on a great event. Think of ways to demonstrate your service in a lively and interesting way – perhaps that's doing a taster class of your offering, a workshop or live demonstration. For example, if you're a yoga teacher, you could put on a complimentary class for journalists and partner with other brands to bring the event to life – think delicious food and drink, an amazing goodie bag or a special performance at the event.

Partnerships can be very valuable with events. If you can partner with other brands that will bring their own audience, contacts and social media following, it will help increase the reach and visibility of the event. Of course, it's worth mentioning that you should only really partner with other brands that align well with yours so think about what businesses would be best for this. A question to consider is: does this brand represent similar values to the ones I have? Does our ethos align with theirs? Do we share a mission?

Get creative with the ways you showcase your brand. Press don't want to give up their precious time going to an event if it's going to be boring, so think outside the box! And don't forget to develop ways to incentivise press to attend – whether that's offering free transportation, complimentary experiences or hospitality. Don't jump into planning an event for the sake of it; really know what your event goals are and how you want a journalist to feel after your event.

TOP TIPS:
PLANNING A SUCCESSFUL PRESS EVENT

Planning your own press event? Tori Porter is a leading fitness and wellness PR consultant and founder of Tori Porter Communications. Tori works with some of the most exciting and emerging start-ups in the fitness and wellbeing space, from activewear to CBD and boutique gyms. Here she shares her top tips for organising a successful press event:

When you're planning a press event, think: *Would I want to attend this myself? Would I drop things in my calendar, or travel on the tube to go to that?*

Ultimately, press get hundreds of invites and your event really needs to stand out as something they'd love to do. Maybe that's something they might do in their own time anyway, like a fitness or yoga class. Or something they wouldn't do themselves but might love to, like trying an amazing new restaurant, or puppy yoga!

It's also important to think about location and timing. Is the location easy to get to? It's not easy to please everyone, but is it a central location, close to media houses, near a station? Timing wise, I tend to find before work or after work are best. People can find it hard to get out of the office at lunchtime or during work hours, so this should maximise attendance.

What can you do to make your event really stand out? Details are key. Personalisation often works well, whether that's gifting product that guests are able to choose themselves, or printing cute name tags to mark a yoga mat, table place or gym locker.

Tori Porter Communications
https://www.toriportercommunications.co.uk/

CHECKLIST FOR EVENTS

It's not just putting on an event, but everything you do around the promotion of the event that really makes a difference – and this is something that's often overlooked. I've attended hundreds of press events and the ones that stand out in my memory are those where all the small details had been considered, and the organisers led with a social-first strategy to encourage journalists to share on social media. You want to make it as easy as possible to share the event on social media, and for this you need to consider what encourages people to share – whether that's the aesthetics of the event, the content or the exclusive access.

INSIDER TIPS FOR EVENT PLANNING

If you're organising a press event, there are a few things to remember that will really help make the most of your efforts. Here's a checklist from Nikki Kitchen, MD at PR agency Purple Riot, of what to remember when you're putting on an event for the media:

⇨ What's the so what? Why would press want to attend your event? What's the news or hook? Ensuring the event is newsworthy or has a unique concept or product available for review is vital in motivating journalists to attend.

⇨ Make sure you target the right journalists and influencers. There's no use inviting hundreds of people who don't write about your topic or sector. And along with media contacts, think about inviting key influencers who can promote your event across their social platforms.

⇨ As well as having a solid news hook, make sure you have key spokespeople available for interview or comment. Share details with the journalists about who will be available beforehand and what they can contribute.

⇨ Location – Unless you're gifting journalists an all-expenses-paid holiday to Ibiza, then think about the

---

location and how to make it as accessible and attractive as possible. By holding the event somewhere beautiful and unique, you will spark interest and motivate attendance.

⇨ Be creative – Journalists and influencers are craving experiences again after spending so much time at home. So how can you make it extra special? Think about food and drinks options and entertainment, or create beautiful decor and Instagram-worthy elements.

⇨ Make sure that you have press materials to hand. Even if you've sent them out beforehand, have printouts or digital assets available to share quickly if requested.

⇨ Use social media to promote and maximise your event's reach. If press can't attend on the night/day, then sharing social snippets on social media might spark an interest in covering the story or product afterwards.

⇨ Share photography and video after the event. Ensure you capture good-quality content to share with your target media list afterwards. By providing good quality images and assets post-event, you increase the chances of pick-up.

⇨ Connect with your guests post-event. Follow up with influencers and media to gauge feedback and gather post-event press coverage. With lots of photography and video content captured throughout the event, maximise that post-event buzz by resharing candid moments across your social media platforms.

Purple Riot is multi-award-winning Manchester-based PR agency established for ten years. They work with a mix of exciting B2C and B2B sectors including hospitality, leisure and lifestyle.

https://purpleriot.co.uk/

PRESS TRIPS

If you have something to offer that you'd like a journalist to experience first-hand, then you might want to consider putting on a press trip. A press trip offers journalists the chance to gain first-hand experience and can take the form of individual or group trips, with other writers.

Press trips often involve international travel, such as promoting a hotel, destination or special event. Group trips often happen around major world events, such as big sporting occasions, or to promote a new destination or hotel openings. Press trips can also happen to promote a destination or show a different side to a city. (I once did a press trip to Geneva to promote the 'affordable side of Geneva', and let me tell you this for free: there is no affordable side to Geneva.)

Trips are a great idea if you have the budget to pull them off. The best way to get coverage is to facilitate a journalist experiencing something for themselves and having an amazing experience that gives them plenty to write about. It's much more dynamic and interesting than sending out a press release and you'll most likely get a much more in-depth feature out of it if you're able to offer them something to experience first-hand.

Press trips pretty much disappeared during the pandemic, but they are coming back in a big way as journalists are more keen than ever before to experience things themselves and start living fully again!

I would give the same advice for press trips as with press events: don't forget the importance of social media around the trip. You want to amplify the opportunity in the moment while you've got journalists there, so make sure that the social media details for the brand or experience are very clear and promoted, to encourage journalists to share the experience on social media. You might want to create a unique hashtag for the trip as a way of collating all the social media sharing and measuring the reach of the trip.

Here's some more advice on putting on a brilliant press trip:

⇨ **Find the right mix of people** – Think about the mix of journalists, influencers or bloggers you want on the trip. You want it to be fun and easy, too, so pick people you think might gel well together, perhaps people of the same age, demographic or who have shared interests. It makes a big difference to the trip if everyone gets along! Of course, you want to make sure this meets your goals in terms of coverage too, but thinking about the group dynamic for a bigger trip is always a good idea.

⇨ **Be very organised with travel plans** – A badly organised press trip is a nightmare, and I've been on plenty of those. You want your trip to be super organised so there's no additional stress or miscommunication during it, so the journalists can sit back and enjoy the experience they are supposed to be writing about. The last thing you want is them worrying about the details of the trip itself, when they should be compiling a story to write.

⇨ **Always provide an itinerary** – Ideally you'd be able to provide this a few days before the trip so they have a clear idea of what's in store and some time to get excited! Make sure all the travel arrangements are very clear and leave some space in the schedule for a journalist to explore and relax in their own time.

⇨ **Have a clear target** – Know why you're hosting a press trip and what you're trying to get out of it. Also get comfortable talking about your client or the experience you're promoting and be able to answer any questions with ease to help support their story-writing.

⇨ **Make it personal if you can** – If you're able to do a personalised trip for a journalist or allow them to bring along a guest, do. Sometimes bringing along a guest is the difference for a journalist wanting to come, as it helps it feel less like 'work' for them. I'll usually say yes to something if I get to bring a friend along!

⇨ **Do your research** – Make sure the journalist you're inviting is the best fit for the experience. If you're offering something of value, don't waste the opportunity on an outlet that isn't the right fit for your brand!

⇨ **Don't jam-pack** a trip with too much to do! The temptation can sometimes be to offer up lots of different experiences and cram things in on a press trip, but journalists also want to enjoy themselves. Better to make a schedule that's a lot more relaxed and enjoyable for everyone.

⇨ **Find ways to incentivise** them to come – do your research into a journalist's interests and see what they have covered before. For example, if you're a pet food brand, why not organise a pet-themed trip to a special dog-friendly hotel in the UK with dog-loving journalists. Get creative with the ways you work with the media!

⇨ **Guarantee the coverage before you go** – A pretty common mistake, but you both need to be on the same page about what you're getting in exchange for the trip. Get the coverage confirmed in writing beforehand, so there's no confusion or awkwardness afterwards. You're well within your right to ask about audience and social media numbers of the publication; this is pretty standard practice if you're inviting them to something of value. Most publications will have a recent media pack they can share in advance of the trip so you've got a good idea of their demographic and reach.

⇨ **Be prepared for things to go wrong** – I've been on plenty of trips where things have gone wrong: I once went on a press trip to Japan for the Rugby World Cup, only for there to be a typhoon, a local lockdown and we spent the whole weekend inside the hotel bar. Be flexible and mindful that not everything will go to plan on a trip, but it's how you deal with it that counts!

GIFTING: YOUR PRODUCT

If you have a product-based business, you may want to send out your products to press. This is called a press drop or press gifting, where products are sent complimentary for review or inclusion in an article. Press drops may feature multiple brands – if, for example, you're doing a Pancake Day-themed press drop, you may want to include multiple brands within one package.

Gifting is a great idea for securing coverage, as it's hard to write about products if you haven't tried them first-hand.

Again, the advice for press trips applies here: figure out the coverage if you're sending something out of value beforehand, and it's a good idea to gauge a journalist's interest before sending it out. Journalists are often bombarded with free stuff and you want to make the most of your gifting budget, especially if you're a small business, and make sure it's not a wasted opportunity.

Also, make sure you have the right address! This may sound basic but in the age of Covid, lots of journalists are working remotely so it's always a good idea to check first.

TOP TIPS:
HOW TO GIFT THE PRESS

Thinking about sending your products out to journalists? Here are some tips from Tori Porter on how to make the most out of gifting products:

Similar to events, great gifting involves thinking about what you would *love* to receive. First, think about the product.

Is the product something that's desirable and potentially something they might not buy themselves? Maybe it's pricey or a luxury. If it is, it's likely going to be a desirable gift anyway.

If it's something that can be harder to tempt people with, like a supplement that you have to try before you realise how much you love it, then you might need to think a little more about what might make this gift desirable. I've been on both the giving and receiving ends of gifting. I've been offered a vitamin D supplement before, something I might have ignored had they not offered a 'wake-up lamp' too, something I'd love to try out but might not get around to buying myself. Think outside the box. If it's a sleep supplement or product, can you send some related items like an eye mask, candle and book?

Adding personalisation makes a gift more special and thoughtful. That might be the gift plus a cookie with their name on, a monogrammed product, or even letting press choose the product to make it more desirable and standout. For example, if it's clothing or jewellery, unless you are pushing a particular item, it might be nice to let the individual choose something to their personal taste.

Packaging is also a big consideration. There's often backlash for gifts that come in a lot of unnecessary packaging. Try to limit that, but also think about how you might be able to send it in a more sustainable manner. There are lots of recyclable materials available, for example, biodegradable packing peanuts that can be dissolved completely in water.

I personally like to check in with press for their address before sending. It avoids waste and frustration at being sent something they didn't want or need. Be courteous and don't push for or expect coverage. The more thought you put into the gift, the more likely you'll see it on social media or receive coverage further down the line. Gifting is ultimately about allowing press to try your product and spreading brand awareness; they will get around to featuring it if and when they can, and the gift will help keep your brand front of mind.

https://www.toriportercommunications.co.uk/

GIFTING: YOUR SERVICES

If you're a service-based business, you may also want to consider gifting to journalists by letting them experience your offering first-hand.

This could come in lots of forms perhaps you can offer a

taster session of your work, a free experience, a complimentary class or course. Lots of coaches will offer free sessions to the press or put on a taster-style class in a group setting. Obviously you don't want to be giving up a lot of your time for free, but if there's guaranteed coverage out of it, then it can be worth it over doing lots of press outreach on email.

Depending on your area of expertise, there are lots of creative ways to get press involved. Try to think of how you're able to offer something off the page which is interesting and would make a great story.

Work out what you're really trying to achieve by offering them something first-hand and how you'd like them to feel. Offering a complimentary service is also a great relationship-builder with the press, and if you have the budget to offer something, it can be used to meet with them face to face. There are two main benefits of gifting an experience as I see it: firstly, you're giving the journalist something to write about, which may lead to press coverage, and secondly, you're able to gather testimonials which are very useful for your business long-term.

A testimonial from a high-profile journalist is a very valuable thing and can benefit you in lots of ways, especially for building credibility and authority within your industry. It can be worth inviting press to experience something for the testimonial alone, even without getting coverage.

TOP TIPS:
GETTING GREAT TESTIMONIALS FOR YOUR BUSINESS

Want to get amazing testimonials for your business? Lisa Johnson is a business strategist who helps ambitious people create passive and semi-passive income streams. In 2021, Lisa had the biggest launch of any UK coach, making £1 million during a masterclass and £2.5 million in total in one week. Here's some insights from Lisa on how to get amazing testimonials to promote your work:

Testimonials are a necessary endorsement of your work.

They are social proof that you are what you say you are. Especially during times of global and financial uncertainty, your customers being able to trust you is of utmost importance.

Why testimonials are important
Testimonials show other potential customers that your product or service is worth having. It shows the results others have got from using it or working with you and allows the new customer to make an informed decision to buy from you.

If your testimonials show happy customers, others will want to be one too.

How to get great testimonials
Before you chase for testimonials, ensure you've delivered what you said you were going to deliver. Provide a great service and the testimonials will naturally be coming in without a need to chase.

Making up testimonials is unethical, and people will see straight through it so don't add stock photos or fake reviews to your marketing. If you need to do that, you should be reconsidering the value you bring to your customers.

Here's how to get great testimonials

1. **Ask for them!** Don't expect people to be falling over themselves to give you good feedback. We all know how loud people complain when something isn't right, but it takes a real effort to share when a business has done something well. Make sure you have plenty of opportunities for people to leave reviews. Make it really easy for them; you could request them via marketing emails, invoices and ask within your social media network. If there is someone you really want to leave you a testimonial, don't be scared to ask!

2. **Share them everywhere.** Make sure when you do receive testimonials you are sharing them everywhere you can,

particularly next to call-to-action points on your website and on social media. When you share more of something, you are more likely to attract more business without the need to keep asking. If you see people leaving a comment about your business on social media, feel free to screenshot and use those too; don't think you have to have a perfectly written testimonial piece.

3. **Offer a reward.** It can often help to offer something in return for a testimonial. Perhaps if they leave a testimonial on your Google or Facebook page, they'll receive a discount or a small bonus next time they shop (so you both benefit!). Just make sure you are very clear in your marketing that you offer a loyalty bonus or discount for testimonials so new customers know. It's all about integrity.

Lisa Johnson
https://www.lisajohnson.com/

Gisela Lyshetti, digital marketing specialist at Market Forever Ltd, has some further tips to add to this:

Receiving great testimonials is the most powerful marketing strategy. This type of marketing is also known as 'reputation marketing' or 'word of mouth', where a business creates a brand ambassador for their product or service. You can ask clients, staff or contractors for testimonials of your service, your commitment and the work produced. This allows prospective customers to understand your core values and your unique selling points.

There are seven simple steps to obtain a great testimonial from a client or your staff:

1. *Mention the intention to obtain a great testimonial from the client at an early stage of your conversation.*

2. *Practise what you preach. Work with your clients to help them reach their business goals and show your commitment, service and loyalty.*

3. *Give them an option. Be aware that not all clients have access to the standard channels to review you. Therefore, it is advised to send a variety of options that they can choose from.*

4. *Timing is everything. As soon as your work is completed and the client is happy, this is your golden moment of opportunity.*

5. *Acknowledge and return the favour. Respond to the review and give the client a review of your collaboration.*

6. *In the event that no testimonial has been given, send a reminder explaining why their feedback is important to you and the business.*

7. *Redistribute your awesome testimonial in other formats such as a video interview, a blog post or a case study that can be used in other settings.*

WORKING WITH INFLUENCERS

Influencer marketing has become one of the biggest trends in the digital space in the last few years; according to eMarketer, there's been a steady growth in the number of marketers using influencers every year, with an estimated 72.5 per cent of marketing campaigns predicted to use influencers in 2022, an increase of 17.1 per cent since 2019.

Now, strictly speaking, a PR plan should focus on earned media – the opportunities you can get for yourself that don't have a cost involved. But the influencer space is something different, and it has become quite the pay-to-play space, which is totally understandable as professional influencers make their money from brand partnerships and have every right to!

So if you're thinking of incorporating working with influencers into your PR plan, it's worth putting aside some budget for this. Even if you're not paying the influencer directly to promote you or provide content for your brand or service, you may have to gift products or give something complimentary, so it's worth budgeting for that.

Influencers can be hugely beneficial to your brand. If you want to spread the word quickly, this is one way to do it. Influencers can tap into a niche for your business and often have a highly targeted following of the ideal customers for you – if you select which influencers to work with wisely.

TOP TIPS:
HOW TO CREATE IMPACTFUL INFLUENCER PARTNERSHIPS

The influencer marketing world is fast moving, and it's good to be ahead of the trends in this space. As head of influencer marketing at leading social media agency Social Chain, Tom Peters devises insight-led influencer campaigns, working with brands including Amazon, Coca-Cola, Lacoste and KFC. Here's his advice on how to successfully work with influencers:

Almost three-quarters of consumers actively avoid advertising – whether that's with ad-blocking technology, by changing their media habits or by subscribing to ad-free streaming services.

People have been losing trust in brands for some time so, to counteract this, brands leaned on influencers to leverage their recommendations and tap into their engaged audiences.

However, the influencer marketing industry has undergone significant change over the last decade, driven largely by technology, culture and shifting consumer values. Feeds are becoming saturated with #ads, audiences are switching off and meaningful engagements with brands are dwindling.

Audiences will still double tap a post, but it's becoming increasingly difficult to cut through the noise and impact purchasing decisions.

But it's not impossible.

Influencers must now live to a new standard – telling human-centric stories with expertise, while demonstrating realism in their output, over historic performance-led and product-driven narratives.

Similarly, brands must work harder. Talent should no longer be seen as an added value to a campaign. Campaign development now needs to be done with an influencer mindset, understanding how talent can weave organically into your branded output from the outset. Integrating truly relevant names to your audience within wider brand campaigns is highly effective and helps elevate your messaging beyond influencers' channels.

If you're reading this and wondering where to begin, I build my approach to influencer marketing in a three-step process:

Understanding and defining objectives, goals and outcomes.

Planning and outreach, ensuring the right tools, platforms and talent are used.

Manage, measure and optimise, safeguarding the brand, building longer-term relationships and delivering consistent results.

Understand and define: All too often, brands fall into the trap of selecting talent that they feel have the right aesthetic for the brand, before understanding the 'why?'

Establishing your objectives for a campaign will help you identify the right talent partners. These objectives will in turn help you develop your audience personas, providing a deeper understanding around who it is you're trying to reach, and how they want you to engage with them.

Devise a strategy that invades the target market's feeds with innovative and engaging content by a variety of influencers;

raising brand awareness of products, tone of voice, and online and in-store offerings while breaking through the noise of competitors' efforts to start to engage brand recall.

Planning and outreach: It's important to ensure that the creator's audience is aligned to your brand as their feed suggests – looking at their demographics, interests and how they interact with the creator. While it can be tempting to compare follower numbers and feed aesthetics, it's this data that will help you understand how the talent's audience might react once they are introduced to your campaign.

Similarly, working with social media influencers should be a collaborative process, avoiding the quick win of a one-size-fits-all output. Influencers can sell product, but they shouldn't be considered social media billboards. They have built their following by understanding what their audience desires. Leverage this deeper understanding to create a bespoke execution. The more personal and creative your brand output is, the more directly it can tie into real stories presented by influencers. Collaborating with a variety of partners across tiers in more niche creative campaigns broken out by product will help to begin to show your brand offerings in a more unique light and build off the brand recall you've initiated in prior campaign pillars.

Manage, measure, optimise: How do you measure and report on the success of your influencer campaign?

I hear it time and again, brand managers executing talent campaigns and demanding almost instantaneous bottom line ROI – all without recognising that creators help support your brand at every stage of the marketing funnel. Depending on where you're playing, and the objectives of the campaign, we can look at different markers of success:

	Top of funnel	Mid-funnel	Bottom of funnel
Behaviour:	Awareness and interest	Consideration and intent	Purchase
Success metric:	Advertising value Content creation value Personification and humanisation	Social connection 3rd party endorsement Emotional value	Retention and loyalty Direct sales Indirect sales

It's only once you have successfully captured an audience's attention – educating them not only on product offerings, but on brand ethos and relevant knowledge within their industry – and only understanding the full consumer journey, that you will be able to successfully lead audiences to engage with the product offering through their preferred method of conversion. This will be dictated by convenience, product availability and price point.

This will become even more prominent in a post-tracking, post-cookie environment, where targeted advertising is replaced with storytelling via a strong branded creative. It's why TikTok creators have grown in popularity so much. The platform lends itself well to relevant, authentic content that allows creators to be their relatable selves. They've nailed making ads that feel as organic and engaging as their business-as-usual content.

Finally, continue to test, learn and optimise. Invest in successful partnerships, and don't be afraid to take learnings from the ones that haven't performed as expected. Social media is an ever-changing network that constantly reinvents, delivering innovative new content formats that help capture audience attention. Understanding how your brand can add value to audiences by leveraging these formats will aid your organic reach and position your brand front of mind for audiences.

KEY TAKEAWAYS:

Think raw and unfiltered first: Engagement in an endless sea of flatlays and unattainable lifestyles has dropped. Consumer appetite has shifted to a more authentic representation and raw output.

Consider influencers at the start of planning, not as an add-on: Developing social media and brand campaigns now should be done with an influencer-first outlook, understanding how talent can weave organically into your brand output from the outset.

Innovation is crucial to engagement: Utilise innovative platforms, formats and features to ensure you stand out in saturated feeds. Engage with talent on their own terms by presenting your narrative and creative ideas before pushing your product.

https://socialchain.com/en

WORKBOK: TAKING YOUR PR PLAN FURTHER

Now we've learnt more about some profile-raising activites you can do for your brand, it's time to get brainstorming. Here are some questions to consider after this chapter:

1. Will you be hosting events to support your PR plan? If so, what kind?

2. Do you have a gifting plan for journalists?

3. Will you be working with influencers within your PR plan?

4. Who are the right influencers for your business?

5. What are you trying to get out of these brand-amplifying activities?

6. Where will you start?

CHAPTER EIGHT

How to Prepare
Your Press Kit

In this chapter, we're going to be looking at the finer details of getting yourself ready for press. From press releases and media kits to high-res photography, there are lots of things to consider so your business is attractive to the media. It's important to be professional here and really show your business in the best possible light.

The ideas and stories are important, but so are some of the more practical materials that you need to pitch and get yourself featured in the media. This is often the part that intimidates people when I work one to one with them – they don't know where to start with putting these materials together and what they are supposed to look like.

So, I'll be running you through what materials you need to get started, and I'll show you some examples of what great press kits look like – and what journalists do and don't like to receive. Getting your business press-ready with high-quality, professional press materials is vital to any PR strategy, as good materials help attach credibility and authority to the pitch.

This chapter will highlight the key press materials you need for your brand, and what journalists want when it comes to photography, bios, press releases and media kits. We'll also be looking at language, which is so important for connecting with journalists and your audience, and how to master it for your business. This chapter will help you get the tone and language of your press materials just right, so you're ready to pitch the press.

WHAT IS A PRESS KIT?

Want to start generating earned media? First you need to create your press kit, which will give journalists all the key information they need about your business to craft a story.

A press kit is, in essence, everything you need to pitch your business out and launch your PR plan. Not every business will need every document I've listed below, but it's a good idea to have an overview of what a journalist may require from you. As an example, standard press kits will include high-resolution images, a press release and a company biography as a starting point, but if you're pitching a founder then you may also want a personal biography, testimonials or a personal quote to give the story more depth.

It's a good idea with a press kit to keep everything in one place: have a Google Drive folder where all the press materials can be found and easily downloaded, or a WeTransfer link. This press folder is invaluable as it makes everything very easy for a journalist and there doesn't need to be lots of back and forth on email to exchange information, which may cost you the story.

Not sure what to include in your press kit? Here's a checklist of the press materials to consider for your business:

⇨ One-liner
⇨ One-page media kit
⇨ Boilerplate
⇨ Imagery
⇨ Biographies
⇨ Press releases
⇨ Mission statement
⇨ Website
⇨ Testimonials

GUIDE: PREPARING YOUR PRESS MATERIALS

Let's dive into each one of these a little deeper and discover together what you need to know about creating these materials:

ONE-LINER

As a starting point, you should be able to summarise your business in one line – both on and off the page.

You want something succinct and clear, ideally sharing what the business does for its customers or demonstrating the company's 'why'. When planning a PR strategy, you also want to make this one-liner something that separates you from your competition. This is often called a strapline or tag line – a short sentence that quickly conveys the message of your brand in as few words as possible.

I would try to use the one-liner as much as possible to get comfortable talking about your business and what it does. You can include the one-liner at the top of a press release, within your company background info and on your social media channels.

PR ONE-PAGER

Something I love to do with my PR one-to-one clients is help them write a really snazzy media kit for themselves. The focus here is profiling the individual behind the business – you can use your personal biography here, but then build on it. This media kit is valuable in advancing your personal brand and gives a taste of what you are uniquely equipped to talk about in the media. It should be presented in a more visually appealing way than simply writing text in an email.

A personal media kit of this kind is very helpful for potential speaking gigs, for sending to broadcast producers, and for trying to secure podcast opportunities. If you're sending out a lot of cold emails to get opportunities, you may find attaching this helps get more responses. It looks professional and gives journalists or event organisers a clear sense of who you are and what you're all about.

What to Include in a PR One-pager

While it might seem a little overwhelming to write a glowing document about yourself for yourself, there's a clear structure and checklist for what to include in your personal one-pager, so don't fear! Here's a rundown of how you'd normally structure a document like this and tips for how to make it stand out:

Start with a tagline for yourself – summarise your job description in five words or less. Mine is 'Entrepreneur and bestselling author'.

Include your name, website address and profile photo – Make sure the photo is a great headshot that represents you well. Choose one that looks professional, but also has some personality. We'll look at personal websites in more depth later, but it's worth mentioning that if you have a separate website for yourself personally as a founder, it's always a good thing.

Short biography – Include a short biography of yourself. You want this to be three hundred words or less so it's not overwhelming to read or too much information on the page. Remember, this is meant to be a snapshot of you as a potential press candidate. Make this sound as impressive as possible, and if you've been featured in the media before, reference it here.

Stats – Include some impressive stats underneath your biography. This might be your monthly website hits, social media stats, business turnover and years of experience in the industry. Again, this document is all about credibility and expertise, and stats can be a great way to convey this.

Press topics – Next, you want to include the most important thing on a media kit: press topics! I'd always suggest having bullet points of three to six things you could confidently talk about in the media, to give a journalist an idea of what your personal expertise and value is.

You can always update these topics over time or tweak them slightly for different opportunities. For example, I have a separate media kit I use for speaking opportunities which is more focused on the things I can speak about and topics I'm often asked to do keynotes on. You want these press topics to be unique to you, but also mainstream enough and appealing to a range of publications; if they are too specific at this stage, you can be narrowing down your press opportunities. Think about what's happening in the world right now and make sure these press topics are relevant and newsworthy with the wider context of the media landscape. Think about what journalists might be writing about in the coming months and choose press topics that are likely to get pick up.

Expertise – I tend to also include some top-line headers of the topics again, as a bullet point list, just in case someone is skim-reading the document. These are essentially soundbites of the topics you can talk about in the press, such as 'Entrepreneurship', 'Dating' or 'Music trends'.

Awards – If you've received any awards, list them here. Even things you were shortlisted for are worth mentioning.

Contact – Make sure your contact details are super visible at the end of the document and don't forget to put links to your social media accounts also.

Previous press – If you've had any press before, this is a great place to include it. I would take screenshots of the press and include this on its own page, selecting the most high-profile press coverage you've had. Similarly, if you've been featured on any podcasts or have spoken at any prestigious events, you could include a page with these. It's a good idea to include a few more photos to finish the media kit, you might want these to be you in situ, such as speaking on stage or receiving an award – anything that paints you in a positive light.

Sample One-pager

You want to make this personal media kit visually attractive and bring some personality to it. Design website Canva is a great place to make an easy media kit template and you can keep adding to it as your visibility in the press grows. Here's an example of my media kit for inspiration:

ENTREPRENEUR + AUTHOR

ANGELICA MALIN

WWW.ANGELICAMALIN.COM

Angelica Malin is Editor-in-Chief of About Time Magazine, one of the UK's leading lifestyle sites. An award-winning entrepreneur & bestselling author of *#SheMadeIt, a toolkit for female founders in the digital age* + *Unattached: Essays on Singlehood*, Angelica is a fresh voice for female empowerment in the UK.

Featured in Forbes, Real Business, Business Insider & the Times, Angelica is a regular commentator on TV and radio on entrepreneurship, start-ups & women in business. She's featured on LBC, Sky News and TalkRadio as a business expert. Her next book, *The PR Bootcamp*, will be out in November 2022.

110K
FOLLOWERS ON SOCIAL MEDIA

80K
MONTHLY WEBSITE HITS

TOP 4
BESTSELLING BOOK

PRESS TOPICS

- The female entrepreneurship boom - why now is the time for female-owned businesses

- Building a personal brand on social media + prediction of digital trends

- Launching your own business - everything you need to know

- Modern dating - why the single positivity movement is thriving

- Lifestyle topics - what's happening in London, emerging trends and insider insights

- Portfolio careers + the future of work post-pandemic

EXPERTISE

Female entrepreneurship
PR + personal brand
Start-ups + modern careers
Future of work

AWARDS

WATC Rising Star Award 2019
BSME Editors' Editor of the Year 2019

CONNECT

07766917484
angelica@abouttimemag azine.co.uk
angelicamalin.com

PRESS FEATURES

- **Real Business** - '10 inspiring UK women-owned businesses'

- **Inc.** - '5 books for small business owners wanting to scale their companies'

- **Jewish Chronicle** - 'How to turn "fluff" into fortune' and 'Unattached at 30? Don't fear life alone'

- **Guardian** - *Unattached* edited by Angelica Malin review

- **Management Today** - 'If you're feeling like an impostor, it's because you probably are'

- **Vogue Australia** - 'All the single ladies' *Unattached* review

- **Cosmopolitan** - 'Books that celebrate love in all its forms'

- **Huffington Post** - '9 books that will change the way you think about love, sex and relationships'

- **Metro** - 'How to be your own work coach and beat burnout'

- **Marie Claire** - 'Female entrepreneurs every woman should follow on Instagram'.

- **New Statesman** - 'How a new wave of literature is reclaiming spinsterhood'

FEATURED PODCASTS

- **The Winging It** Podcast with Lucy Hitchcock

- **Alonement** with Francesca Specter

- **A Single Serving** with Shani Silver

- **Hashtag Authentic** with Sara Tasker

- **Start the Week** - BBC Radio 4

- **Strategically Winging It** with Sonya Barlow

- **Creator Journals** with Kimberly Spiers

- **Creative Rebels** with David Speed and Adam Brazier

- **She Can. She Did.** with Fiona Grayson

- **The Co-Working Club** with Jessica Berry

BOILERPLATE

Boilerplate is a fancy term for some copywriting text that you use on different marketing materials. In a PR context, this template of text is useful to have when sending journalists the key information about your business. It's essentially a stock set of copy that can be very handy for pitches and press release.

Boilerplate text tends to be two to three paragraphs long, and will include the company background, key information and any recent stats, awards or accolades. You don't want to overload with details in the boilerplate text, but you do want to give journalists everything they need for a story. It's not as comprehensive as a press release or an 'About Us' section on a website, but offers a summary of the business and its mission.

IMAGERY

Imagery is very important for your PR outreach, and investing in good quality photography will make a world of difference when pitching. Very often the quality of the images sells a story, especially for something visual or aspirational like travel, food or luxury experiences.

You want to have a range of photography available, including both landscape and portrait photos (different websites will have different styles they like). Photography should always be high-resolution, for potential use in print publications, and a mixture of candid and more high-end brand images is a good idea.

If you have a product-based business, you'll probably want to invest in both product images and more lifestyle shots, with the product in situ. Avoid anything that looks too staged – you want to show your product in real life, how it would actually be used by customers. Some publications don't like photos that are too obviously branded, so try to avoid these and instead offer some more lifestyle photos which are less clearly brand-focused.

Imagery of the individuals behind the business is also very important and should not be overlooked. You want headshots for any potential interview features, events or podcast promotion in the future; headshots are often the first thing a journalist will ask for after they have written a story, so make sure you invest in some good ones every six months or so. You can also use these across your social media platforms to give your work and concept a polished, professional feel. Headshots should represent you in your best light; also think of what kind of person you want to attract to your work, and style your photography around your ideal client.

FIVE TIPS FOR STAND-OUT BRAND PHOTOGRAPHY

Want to show your brand in the best possible light? Lydia Collins is a London-based professional brand photographer and content creator. Below she shares her tips on how to make your business shine through standout photography.

When it comes to brands, there's nothing more important than epic brand photography. It's a way brands communicate with their customers, show their identity and ultimately generate sales. Here are my top tips on how to enhance your brand photography:

1. **Have a vision.** Before any shoot, it's essential that the photographer understands the brand, the brief and their creative visions. Providing visuals for your photographer is key. Create a mood board based on what you want to achieve and have visual cues to show the photographer the aesthetic you're trying to achieve. Have a clear understanding of this before the shoot – make sure everyone on set is visually aligned, as this saves a lot of time and leaves room for the photographer to experiment. Don't be afraid to let the photographer bring different ideas to the table, and try adding colour, experimenting with shooting angles and lighting set-ups. The main focus is to create those power shots that draw in consumers. This leads me to the next tip ...

2. **Create personality and relatable content within your images.** Your images will perform the best when you create

relatable content. When it comes to brand photography, consumers want to see personality and they want to see relatability. Generating a story is a great way of doing this. Incorporating a human element is another great way, whether this is the use of hands, hair or a full body. For example, if you were shooting jewellery, show it being used! The consumer wants to know how good that piece of jewellery will look on them. If you're shooting a dress, show that dress moving, show how it can look on the potential consumer. Even if the brand involved isn't something you can wear, you can still add a human element. Think of a flatlay-type image of a beauty product – a hand coming in from one edge of the corner as if they are about to grab the product not only shows the consumer the size of the product but it makes it relatable – they want to be able to see themselves having this product.

3. **Lighting and location.** Probably one of the most important aspects when it comes to not just branding photography but any photography is lighting. Lighting is key when it comes to creating those eye-catching power shots. We live in a world where everything is so quick – you want to be able to blow people away from that very first moment they see your photos, so having your lighting planned prior to the shoot is key. If you're using natural light and shooting outside, you want to be checking the weather and making sure you're shooting at the right time of day that suits you. For example, if you're after a warm glow for a fashion or beauty shoot, you want to make sure you're shooting in morning or evening light when the sun is lower in the sky.

    If you're shooting within a studio and using artificial lighting, you want to think about where this lighting is hitting the product, clothing or model's face, and make sure that it isn't unflattering or creating shadows that could distract the viewer. Location is another aspect that is often overlooked but I've found it to be a make or break on shoots. You want the location to enhance the brand you're shooting; it needs to align with the brand and what you or they are trying to convey. For example, if you're shooting a swimwear brand, think about the location and how this can enhance the visuals – does having palm trees in the background align with the brand and their messages? Or are they a brand that focuses more on the swimwear being used, in which case, is a location where water is visible a necessity?

4. **Props can really make an image**, turning a very simple photograph into *that* shot. Find props that resonate with the brand you're shooting – these can be props that match the brand's colour, props that would accentuate the brand you're shooting or props that are simply there to enhance the usability of the brand. For example, if you were shooting a campaign for a beauty brand, using flowers that match the pops of colours on the model's face can massively enhance the final shot. Naturally, we're more drawn to photography that resonates with us because we envision it in our lives. The props also don't have to be small! If you're shooting a high-end fashion brand for an editorial, you could use props such as horses, cars or palm trees – the possibilities are endless!

5. **Poses and directing your model.** If you're working with models, you want to be able to direct them into poses that best suit the brand you're shooting. This goes back to creating personality within a photo that I touched on earlier; if you can direct your model in a way where it's creating an eye-catching image and also making the brand you're shooting relatable, you're onto a winner. Think about moving arms around, having them lifted above the model's head, placing them on their hips, getting your model to crouch

down low in order to get a close-up shot. Don't be afraid to experiment, try new poses out and make your model feel comfortable by showing them the poses yourself. Remember: a comfortable and happy model always makes for better images.

Most importantly, enjoy yourself and let your creativity flow! Experiment with different props, poses, angles to find what best suits the brand you're shooting. Try and test different set-ups and locations – whether these be at home, photography studios or street locations. Spend time familiarising yourself with your kit and you'll be ready to take on any brand or nail your own branded shots in no time!

BIOGRAPHIES

Biographies are important, and writing a great biography is a skill. It's something a lot of people I coach one to one find difficult, as we tend to undersell ourselves and get a bit shy talking about achievements, but PR is all about bigging yourself up and showing your business in the best possible light.

Sometimes I find it helpful to get a third party to look over a biography and give advice on how you're coming across – this can be a colleague, friend or former boss. This is helpful as often it's difficult when you've spent a lot of time writing something to see it properly and you can overwork it too. A third party may be able to tell you how the copy is sounding and give you some pointers on things to change.

It's a good idea to always have two biographies to hand when PR pitching:

Personal biography – Around eight hundred words about the founder, which includes some biographical information about them personally, their journey or career history which can be used for pitching. Include any interesting details, such as education, career history, motivation, awards, accolades, plus any personal circumstances or details that led them to where they are today. It's a good idea to use the same biography on LinkedIn, so there's a consistency between platforms and you can also use it in your personal press kit.

Here's an example of personal biography that works well:

Amanda Fitzgerald is passionate about all things entrepreneurial having been brought up by parents who ran their own businesses. Inevitably, she followed in their footsteps and in 2008 she set up her first business, a luxury online knitwear store importing ethically produced alpaca knitwear from Peru. Remembering her mother's successful £1m turnover mail-order business's launchpad: a small mention in the *Daily Mail* that literally catapulted her business to the hearts and minds of the public, Amanda set about securing press coverage for her knitwear brand. She secured features and mentions in glossies and nationals. She was then asked by friends and colleagues to do the same for their businesses and so her PR consultancy was born. She now shares her PR secrets with ambitious and inspirational entrepreneurs as she trains them on how to succeed at media pitches so they can be seen everywhere.

Company biography – Around one thousand words about the company, sharing key information such as its purpose and history. In this biography, you can go a little more in depth than in other parts of the press materials and flesh things out more. Remember to keep it personal and colourful – biographies don't need to be a boring read and you can still inject some life into things.

A good company biography is something you can repurpose for lots of different situations, so it's worth investing time and energy into this to make it just right. You want to make sure this biography is always kept up to date with any changes within the company and that you're using the same one across comms, including on your website.

If you're struggling to make it impactful, go back to the purpose of your business. Think about your desired audience and how you're helping people – especially if you're a new start-up. You want to focus on what the company's purpose is: Who does it serve? How does it serve these people?

MISSION STATEMENT

While this isn't a total prerequisite to include in a press kit, I do think it's always helpful to have a mission statement handy for journalists. It can help situate your business in the context of what's happening in the world and thus make it more newsworthy, especially if it's anything to do with sustainability, social change or politics.

A mission statement is normally 500–800 words and succinctly shares the core message and ethos of your business. This statement will draw you back to the 'why'. A successful mission statement is impactful and clear in its vision. Context is so important in journalism; we want to see the context of why the business exists, what change it's trying to bring about and how it's doing this.

PRESS RELEASES

A press release is a document you'll use for pitching a news story – you won't always need a press release for the business, but if you have some news to announce, this is the best format to do so.

A press release is useful if you're announcing a new partnership, a new business launch, fundraising or have anything else that's new and noteworthy to share. We'll be looking in more detail at how to write a great press release in the next chapter, but for now, note that it's useful to have one ready to go within your press kit.

PERSONAL WEBSITE

A well-designed website that's set up for press opportunities can do wonders for your business. Always include a link to your website within your press kit, on a press release, a personal media kit or at the end of your biography. I would advise to have a separate website for you personally as a founder, alongside your company one.

TOP TIPS:
CREATING A PRESS-FRIENDLY WEBSITE

Not sure where to start? Here are some tips for crafting a great website that catches the eye of a journalist and converts into coverage:

➪ **Keep it consistent** – by this I mean, have a consistent colour and theme. The more professional looking the website, the more credible you'll seem to the media. Use the same colours on your personal media kit and on social media. You can design a brand kit in Canva and pick colours that you'll keep using across platforms and documents.

➪ **Imagery** – use high-quality imagery on your website. Be strategic with the imagery you choose; if you're trying to get more speaking opportunities, then include photos of you speaking on stage. If you're trying to get more podcast opportunities, get a photo of you in a recording studio.

➪ **Video content** – if you have any videos of you, include them! A video of you talking about your business or work is going to be so much more effective than static text and, again, if you have any videos of you doing something that's aligned with your work goals, such as speaking, then include them.

➪ **Have a stand-out press section** – you want a press section on the website that is clear and easy to find. You want to include all your recent press and keep this updated every time you get a new piece of coverage. It should be visible from the homepage and included in the navigation bar. Journalists will often look to see if you've been featured in other publications as a way of checking your credibility, so you want to maximise any opportunities you do get.

⇨ **Make it easy to get in touch** – forget contact forms, they are off-putting. Have your email clearly listed on the website and make it super easy for a journalist to get in touch. You may also want to have a link to your Google Drive press folder directly on the website with all your press materials so a journalist can easily download this – it can act as your own personal media centre.

TESTIMONIALS

If you've got great client testimonials, then there's no harm in including them in a press kit. I would collate all the testimonials onto one page and save them as a Word document for easy access. Having high-profile quotes from other journalists would be valuable too, and if you've got any testimonials from super high-profile individuals, such as celebrities, then consider including these on a press release or within a company overview.

SUMMARY:
WHAT TO INCLUDE IN A PRESS FOLDER

To summarise this, within your press folder, you want to include:

⇨ Company background information, such as biographies, mission statement and boilerplate text
⇨ High-resolution imagery
⇨ Logos for the business
⇨ Contact details
⇨ Anything that supports your business' credibility, such as awards and a page of collated testimonials
⇨ A personal media kit (one-pager) if you're pitching the founder as well

---

TOP TIPS:
MASTERING LANGUAGE AND TONE FOR YOUR BUSINESS

Not sure how to talk about your business in the right way? It can be tricky to prepare these press materials if you're not sure about the tone and language that your business should be using – you want it to be authentic and personal to you, but still professional. Here, freelance brand strategist and writer Rebecca Magnus shares her insights on how to get the tone just right for your business:

When it comes to mastering tone and language for your business, what factors should you consider?
First of all, don't think about tone. When thinking about language for your business, it's far more valuable to focus on the principles of good writing. In a nutshell, that's thinking about what you have to say, what your audience wants to know, and saying that in the way that feels right. It's a more intuitive way to write, and it will lead to better communication, and far more interesting conversations.

Writing is a craft in its own right. Here are some basic principles to start you off:

Write how you speak. Relax your tone: use shorter words, contractions, mimic the ebb and flow of conversation with a balance of longer and shorter sentences. Treat your reader like you would a friendly acquaintance, warm, welcoming and respectful.

Write for your reader. Every piece of copy has an intended audience. To write well, you need to understand who your audience is and how what you're writing can benefit them, whether that's dropping a new product line or simply posting a meme for a smile. Why are you writing? What's in it for the reader? Why should they care? Always consider your audience when you write.

Get to the point. Whenever you're writing, think about why you're writing. What do you want to happen next? It could be as simple as to encourage engagement on a social media post or make a purchase on an online shop. Whatever it is, tell people what you want them to do. Then make it easy for them to do it.

Consistency matters. Be consistent in your writing style. Don't write in a super chatty tone on social media then send stand-offish, corporate sales emails. It feels weird, disjointed and uncomfortable. It makes a brand feel inhuman, a construct rather than a human enterprise.

Flexibility also matters. While consistency is important, don't forget you can flex your style for context. Dealing with customer complaints in a chatty, informal and jokey voice would feel inappropriate. Likewise, writing Instagram posts with business jargon would be an odd choice. It's all about balance.

As we develop more awareness of our own subconscious biases and systemic oppression of marginalised groups, it's become more important than ever that brands write in an inclusive way to increase accessibility for everyone. This is a huge subject, however here are a couple of thought starters:

Write inclusively for your audience. This means use simpler language (lay off the idioms for non-native speakers), try to use non-gendered and non-discriminatory language and inclusive terms where possible. This is particularly important for the disabled community, as many common phrases are considered 'ableist'. Do your research into preferred terms when addressing the needs of a particular community. If you're unsure whether a term you're using is appropriate, ask a member of that community, hire a sensitivity reader, or find another word to convey the idea.

Make accessibility a priority. Wherever your writing appears, make sure that there are accessible options for people to read the information in a variety of formats, including Braille, video and BSL. This is particularly important on social media, where a couple of simple tweaks can make your content more accessible, including image captions for screen readers, and live captions on videos for d/Deaf people.

How do you go about crafting tone for a business? Where do you start?

When I write for a brand, I don't think about tone. I start with questions. What makes this brand distinctive? Who is the audience? How can we make it compelling and memorable? How do we resonate with the right people? How do we cut through the noise? What's the context of the brand and communication touch point, and how can I use that to make the message memorable? What information is useful to the reader? What's the one message they need to know?

I ask these questions of everyone who might seem relevant. And, sometimes, people who seem irrelevant. I'm curious as to the answers, particularly the unexpected ones. I'm genuinely interested in people, what they do and why they do things. Throughout my investigations, I'm always writing. I record observations, facts, feelings, random tangents, serendipitous findings and anecdotes in a scruffy notebook. Beware the lure of the beautiful notebook – you'll never write anything in it. Cheap, battered pads you don't mind ripping pages out of work best I've found. By the end of this exercise, I have reams of notes. This is my foundation for developing tone.

I'm then ready to play with words. It's an exercise that's

equal parts enjoyable and frustrating. Words often misbehave. I think about the idea behind the words. What are we really trying to convey? I think about what every line needs to do and where it will go. Should it grab the reader by the collar and pull them in? Should it highlight the benefits of a particular product or service? I think about how I want the reader to feel. Should they feel a rush of excitement, a flash of self-confidence or a blush of vulnerability? Branding is not logical. It is visceral and emotional. Our words don't only make logical arguments, they speak to our deepest desires and fears. And sometimes, they just sell soap. Through playing with words in answer to deep and banal questions, ideas surface and a tone emerges. It's an organic, fluid and strange process.

Any advice on how brands can sound more 'authentic' and what that even means?

Brand authenticity is much more than tone of voice; it's everything the business does. That's why establishing values at the outset and using them for decision-making in every aspect of business matters. In terms of tone, the principle is simple: say what you mean, and mean what you say. If you're making a tough decision, tell people about it, and why you're doing it. Let people in on your thinking, let them be part of your journey. By sharing the good, the bad and the ugly (within reason) in language that connects with people, you can begin building that all-important community that will help to carry you through the bad times and the good.

What does 'good' copy look like to you?

Good writing is deceptively simple. It's clear. It condenses a complex idea or emotion into a few words. It uses new imagery, or twists a common cliché into something new. It resonates with the right people. It makes you think. It makes you feel. Sometimes it evokes a tear, and sometimes a smile. Often, it doesn't take itself too seriously, but it always gets the point across. It does the job it needs to do, nothing more, nothing less. And it sticks in the mind like glue.

It is hard to write good copy.

What common mistakes do you see brands making with their copy?

Many brands try far too hard. Either they are desperate to be the next Oatly or Innocent, and slavishly copy those tones of voice, or they piggyback off the latest TikTok craze to chase likes and engagement above building community. There's nothing wrong with taking inspiration from other brands or using memes, but when you chase instant validation and gratification to the detriment of writing anything useful for your audience, it creates a brand voice that feels robotic, inhuman and fake. YAAAAS QUEEN is not a personality trait, and it does not make for good brand communication.

This is often a symptom of a bigger problem: they do not understand their brand or their audience. When you don't understand what you stand for, why you're different and who your audience is, it's understandable why you'd panic, blindly copy trends, and do anything to get a bit of traction. But it's not the best way to build a brand for the short, medium or long term. Exploring and expressing the things that make you you, and connecting with the right people, is a difficult but worthwhile journey. And it always leads to better copy at the end. It's hard to ask the tough questions, but when businesses are struggling to articulate themselves, that's where I always start. With hard questions, an open mind and a scruffy notebook.

How important is copy in a PR strategy?

PR is all about telling a compelling story in a way that grabs attention and media space. Brand is about creating distinction in the mind of the consumer and making your brand memorable to the right people. The common thread between the two is establishing relevancy and grabbing the attention of the right audience. Strong narrative and messaging can help do that.

When developing a verbal identity, aka a tone of voice, I would normally write a brand narrative and key messaging. A strong narrative tells the stories about the brand in a compelling way. This might be the founding story, craft stories around process, or stories around sourcing and creating products. Every brand is bursting with stories they can tell, brand narratives hone the most important ones to communicate. As a starting point, PR strategies can take these stories and find newsworthy angles to widen their audience and grow their community.

Then we come to key messaging. This refers to the most important messages a brand needs to communicate about their product or business so that people understand what's special about it and why they should buy. These messages often cover a range of topics, including purpose, process and product. With strong key messages established, it should be much easier to find a newsworthy angle on your latest product launch and explain to journalists quickly and simply the relevance of your product, service or brand to their latest round-up or business article.

What tips do you have for stand-out copy on a website?
Put simply, stand-out website copy gets people to do the thing the business wants them to do. It entices people to take action, whether that's signing up to a subscription, buying a product or asking for a quote. It's clear, easy to read and easy to understand. It presents information in a flow that feels intuitive, gives people the facts they need to take action, and makes that action easy to do. For this reason, good user experience (UX) design goes hand in hand with good writing.

Copy that devastates with its intelligence or charm might be fun to read, but if it doesn't communicate clearly or help a business achieve its aims, it's not good copy. Whenever people go on a website, they're trying to achieve something, whether that's find information, make a purchase or get to the next step of the selling process. Good copy makes it easy to do that.

Where do you think the future of brand copywriting is going in the age of Instagram and less traditional advertising forms?
Platforms like Instagram and TikTok have changed the dynamic of relationships between brands and people. It's no longer a passive dynamic between a brand and their audience, but an interactive dynamic between brands and their communities.

For brand writing, that means considering how your tone flexes across two-way interactions, encourages conversation and how your brand reacts to events as they happen. Whether that be a major news event or a viral meme, being proactive in your role and reactive to situations as they happen is important. And for that, I think the key is knowing who you are as a brand, and how you speak inside out. That way, you'll always have something to say and know how to say it.

https://www.rebeccamagnus.co/

WORKBOOK: GETTING YOUR PRESS MATERIALS READY

There's lots of information in this chapter about press materials, so let's look at your personal PR plan and which materials are the most important for you to create:

1. Does your business have a one-line summary you can use?

2. What press materials are the most important for you to create?

3. Do you need a personal media kit too?

4. What kind of language will you use to describe your business?

5. What kind of photography do you need to support your business?

6. What are the highest priority materials to create right now?

7. Do you need a press release for your story?

CHAPTER NINE

How to Write
a Great Press Release

In this chapter, we'll be delving deeper into the topic of press releases, exploring what to include on a press release, what makes a great release and how to get your release in front of journalists.

Of course, there's no point in having a stand-out press release if no one sees it, so we'll be looking at some strategies here for maximum distribution and reach. There's a mixture of approaches you can take for this, either building your own list of contacts or using a distribution wire to send out your release to journalists.

Press releases are often quite overused in media, and it's worth thinking about whether you actually need one before creating the asset. So, let's dive in and look more at press releases – when, why and how to use them:

WHAT IS A PRESS RELEASE?

A press release essentially is an official statement that an organisation or company issues to the media. It's also sometimes called a press statement, a news release or a media release. It's an official news story, often produced by a PR agency, although of course you can produce one yourself – it's fairly straightforward. A press release is one of the key tools to use in your press outreach and is the most common thing used when you want lots of eyeballs on a story, rather than sending out individual pitches.

Good press releases should answer the questions of who, what, why and where of a story – with direct, non-fluffy language and normally a couple of quotes to give the story some context and character.

Press releases are best when they are succinct. They normally run between one and two pages maximum and give just enough information for the publications to be able to run a story, along with images and contact details of the organisation.

Press releases are public and will often be widely shared, so you need to make sure you're totally happy with your release before it goes out and that it's factually accurate. Investors, customers and stakeholders in your company will also be able to see the release, so bear this in mind when writing it. To that end, your release is also a marketing material and should be treated as such – it's not simply something that provides information for a story, but also tells a lot about your company overall. Of course, news coverage is the goal when sending out a press release, but you never know who might see it.

WHEN DO YOU NEED A PRESS RELEASE?

The main thing I want to convey here is that you don't always need a press release for a story, and they are often overused. It can be helpful to have a press release on file about the launch of a company, which can be used if a journalist asks for it, but not every story is worthy of a press release.

While there's no cut-and-dried formula for when to use a press release or what to include on it, there are a couple of different occasions in which you may want to produce one. You'll notice I use the word 'new' a lot here – this is to emphasise that if you're going to send out a press release it should be newsworthy. If it's new, it's more likely to be news.

Here's when and how you might use a press release:

NEW BUSINESS LAUNCHES

If you've recently launched a new business, this is a great time to send out a press release. Include all the key information about the new business offering – what the idea behind it is, who the founders are, what you're trying to achieve, what the business structure or revenue plan is. Don't jump the gun though; often I see businesses wanting to send out a release the week they have launched and actually it's sometimes better to hold fire for a little bit until the business has some momentum, good stats or some customers, as this will make it a better story for the press.

NEW PRODUCT LAUNCHES

A new product launch is also a valuable time to send out a press release. You want to spread the word about what new thing you're offering to consumers, and a release is the quickest way to do that. In a release of this kind, you should place emphasis on the new product's specs, price, when it's available and what's unique about the new product offering. Make sure to include links to high-resolution photography too – both lifestyle and cut-out images.

MERGERS AND ACQUISITIONS

One of the main reasons you would send out a release as a corporate company is in the case of a merger or acquisition. Here you want to explain the organisational change, highlighting the projected growth and trajectory of the company based on this new change. This is a good place to use quotes also. You can include quotes from the senior leadership team on the merger or acquisition, and about what it means for the business.

HIRING

If you've got an exciting new hire, especially at senior level, why not share the news? A press release in this instance would want to pay particular attention to the new hire, including any biographical information, accolades, career history or background. A photo is a good idea, along with any other bits of credibility-boosting information you can include.

PRODUCT UPDATES

You may want to send out a press release if you've updated a product or service recently. Similar to sending out a release about a new business or product launch, this release would give the main information about the product update, its ideation and when the updated product will be available.

AWARDS AND ACCOLADES

Of course, winning an award is a good time to send out a press release. This is one of the few times that bragging rights are allowed – if you've won something, shout about it! On this kind of release, include information about the award, a company biography, along with a personal quote about winning the award and what it means for your business.

NEW OPENINGS

A new opening is the perfect example of when to send out a press release. Whether it's a new restaurant, hotel or destination opening, why not share the news of it with your audience. Include the date and location of the opening, and anything that makes the story special, such as the design team behind a hotel opening, or the chef behind a new restaurant.

NEW PARTNERSHIPS

Partnerships are another good reason to send out a press release. The release for this would be similar to the one you send out in case of a merger or acquiring a business; you would include a summary of each business, the reason for the partnership, its length and expected impact. Go deeper and explain the why of the partnership: what are the two businesses bringing collectively and hoping to achieve?

EVENTS

Event marketing is one of the main reasons you'd send out a press release, and it's standard practice to send out a release before any major sporting, music, literary or international event. Festivals are another time a release would be sent out. You want to be sending out a release at least a few months before a big scale event in order to secure print coverage.

On the release, include information about what the event is about, when and where it will be held, how to attend (is it ticketed or a free event) and photos for the upcoming event (failing this, photos from a previous event of the same kind would work). You may want to include a quote from the event organiser also to give the story some intrigue.

HOW TO WRITE A PRESS RELEASE

There's a common structure to press releases, which, once you get the hang of, will make them super easy to put together. You really don't need to spend on an agency to master this – the format, story and language will make the release press-worthy. Below is a guide on how to structure a press release, and then we'll look a little deeper at what each section of the release should contain.

PRESS RELEASE FORMAT

1. Contact information and 'For Immediate Release' at the top.

2. A main headline and subheading in italics to summarise the news.

3. A location and news hook in the opening line.

4. Two to three paragraphs of further information about the story, with context and more details.

5. Any key facts in bullet points.

6. A company description or personal biography at the bottom.

7. Some symbols to mark the end of the release or 'END'.

PRESS RELEASE STYLE

Language

The purpose of a press release is to share news. As such, the language used should be straightforward and newsy – you don't want anything too flowery or descriptive, but instead you should share the facts and key information in an easy-to-digest way. You essentially want it to be possible for a journalist to copy large parts of the text and use it on their website or publication without too much editing.

Style

As a starting point, every release should have these basic stylistic points:

⇨ Your contact information should be very easy to find. This is normally placed on the top left on a press release.

⇨ The phrase 'for immediate release' placed on the top right.

⇨ An eye-catching headline which gives a clear insight into the announcement and gets the attention of the reader.

⇨ A business location i.e., 'London, United Kingdom'.

⇨ A very succinct and impactful biography at the end of the release which could be used as a stand-alone piece of copy.

⇨ Usually you will include a 'Notes to Editor' section towards the end of the release which has bullet-point facts about the news, in case the journalist is skim-reading it and needs information quickly.

⇨ A signifier that the release is ended.

BODY TEXT
In the body of the release itself, this is what you want to include and why:

Paragraph One

This is where you want to include the attention-grabbing headline and really sell the story. The first paragraph should contain all the key information to make the story stand out and give the journalist everything they need in a short soundbite.

Don't overcomplicate things; tell your story, get to the point and make it relevant. Think about the news too – is there a news hook you can mention in the first line? This will help draw a journalist's eye in.

Paragraph Two/Three

The next two paragraphs should give more reference and colour to the story. This is where you give context, details and use some personal insights to make it more narrative-focused. For example, you may want to include quotes from the CEO or an expert in this section. You're also telling the 'why' in this section, so make that clear from the outset.

Final Paragraph

The last paragraph is usually an 'About Us' section. This is where you would include a company biography or personal one, depending on the release. This is where the facts about the company are shared and you'd normally end with some contact information, a link to images or more information and bullet points of the key details.

WHAT MAKES A GOOD PRESS RELEASE?

Here are some golden rules about writing a good press release:

1. WRITE AN EYE-CATCHING HEADLINE

Headlines need to stand out. You want something that is relevant to the story, but also timely and interesting. You've got to get a journalist's attention from the outset, so make it captivating. Some tips for this:

⇨ Be specific: who, what, why
⇨ Using action words
⇨ Don't overwrite it; one line is perfect

You want to think about both the journalist and the end consumer here – does a journalist have enough to go on to make this a good story for the reader?

2. MAKE IT NEWSWORTHY

Don't forget to make it newsy! Newsjacking, where a brand or company align with a current event or high-profile news story to generate media exposure, is particularly relevant when creating press releases.

The release should take a pyramid structure, from the most important details to the least important. So, the most newsworthy pieces of information should be at the top of the release, in the first paragraph. Make sure the context is covered in the first half of the release, and the 'why' in the second.

3. USE QUOTES TO MOVE THE STORY ALONG

Personal quotes can be a great addition to a press release, but very often they do little to move the story along and will just repeat things already said in the release. If you're going to include a quote, make it interesting! I've seen hundreds of releases that include a quote from the CEO about how delighted they are about a partnership, and that's not interesting!

Don't use up valuable space on the release saying something generic or repeating yourself. I would include a maximum of two quotes in the release, and always try to get a quote from the most senior or relevant person at an organisation.

4. INCLUDE A PHOTO

I personally like a press release that includes high-res photography at the start of the release to give it some flavour. Press releases can be a bit dry, and this is a good way to inject some personality. Especially if your release is about anything with a visual aspect, like food or travel, it will help draw the reader in.

5. ADD NARRATIVE VALUE

Don't forget to include things that strengthen your narrative! Just because it's news, don't overlook the storytelling element. The release should offer a complete story, with its own narrative arc where possible. This might mean mentioning the future implications of this announcement or how it relates to what's happening in the world.

6. USE PLAIN LANGUAGE + KEEP IT SIMPLE

When in doubt, keep it simple. Most press releases are overwritten – you really want to keep it to one page and use super simple language. Try not to be too gushing on a release; it's a journalist's job to decide how good a product or story is, not yours. If you're citing any data or statistics, make sure to reference properly.

To summarise, in my eyes, a good press release:

- Is straight to the point
- Isn't overwritten
- Uses simple language
- Is well fact-checked
- Is information-heavy
- Is newsworthy
- Uses some imagery

PRESS RELEASE EXAMPLE

I know this is a lot of information to take in, so here's an example of a press release in a simple format to copy:

CELEBRATIONS AT THE UK'S FIRST DRIVE-IN WEDDING

FOR IMMEDIATE RELEASE

LONDON, Monday 5 October 2020: A creative Bride and Groom have found a way to still have a Covid-compliant wedding – by staging the UK's first drive-in for over 200 guests at their venue in Essex.

Roma Popat and Vinal Patel from London were originally due to get married on 20th April 2020, but when lockdown disrupted their plans, they suggested their tongue-in-cheek idea to their Wedding Co-Ordinator, Saheli Mirpuri from Saheli Events.

What began as a joke soon became a reality, and on Friday 2nd October 2020, Roma and Vinal were married in front of a small gathering of their immediate family at Braxted Park, Chelmsford. As they said their vows, in an adjacent field to the venue, more than a hundred cars containing friends and family were parked up, watching the ceremony unfold on a big screen.

On arrival at the drive-in wedding, guests were given welcome hampers containing anti-bacterial hand gel and were requested to stay in their vehicles throughout. They were also able to order food from their respective seats through a waiter service delivered directly to them. If they needed any help, they just flashed their lights or hazard flashers.

As is tradition with Hindu weddings, the Groom made an entrance, but this time, he travelled around the field before the ceremony, waving at guests in their cars. Horns were honked as he travelled past on a highly decorated golf buggy, driven by a member of venue staff wearing a protective mask.

After the intimate ceremony inside had been completed, the Bride and Groom then travelled around the field on the same golf buggy, waving to their friends and families at a distance.

Saheli Mirpuri from Saheli Events said: 'We're delighted with how both the ceremony and the UK's first drive-in wedding has gone. This year has been so difficult for luxury Asian weddings and celebrations, but this was a creative way to still ensure that guests felt they were with the couple on the day. We're delighted to have worked with so many amazing suppliers to bring everything together.'

Bride Roma Popat said, 'When we had to postpone our wedding in April, we had no idea whether we would be able to get married this year or not. We have so many friends and family and we wanted them to be part of our celebration. It literally meant everything to us to have everyone there, albeit in a slightly different way to the one we envisaged. It's a day we'll never forget.'

As the weather was fine on the day, the couple were even able to stage their final ceremony in front of the drive-in screen, so their friends and family could see the walk-out element of the day.

For more information or to speak to the Bride and Groom or Saheli Mirpuri from Saheli Events, please contact Nicola Rowley at NJRPR at nicola@njrpr.com

HOW TO SEND OUT YOUR PRESS RELEASE

There are a few key ways to send out a press release. Here are a few options:

BUILD YOUR OWN MEDIA DATABASE

This isn't the quickest route, but in terms of longevity it's the most beneficial. You can create your own little black book of contacts and send out your release this way using newsletter software, such as MailChimp or MailMerger.

USE A NEWSWIRE

There are a few services that are designed for sending out press releases in a pay-to-play format – these are called newswires or press release distribution companies. The best ones globally for doing this are:

⇨ Newswire
⇨ PR Newswire
⇨ Cision
⇨ Business Wire
⇨ Prowly

MEASURING THE REACH OF YOUR PRESS RELEASE

If you're targeting online media, you can measure the reach and impact of your press release based on a few key metrics:

⇨ Click-throughs
⇨ Online articles
⇨ Referrals traffic to your website from the press release
⇨ Referrals from social media or search engine
⇨ Increased backlinks to your website
⇨ Google Alerts around your business

If you're targeting print media, you can measure the reach through the number of print articles written about your business off the back of your release.

CASE STUDY:
NAOMI ACKERMAN ON HOW TO SELL
A BUSINESS STORY

Name: Naomi Ackerman
Age: 30
Job title: Freelance business journalist, previously business reporter at the *Evening Standard*, reporting on tech and the hospitality, leisure and travel sectors.

What's the best way to catch an editor's eye with a PR pitch?

Make sure the pitch is exclusive, has a great top line, and contains all the information a journalist writing a story on the topic would need to know.

Just like any business owner, editors are on the lookout for anything that makes a mark and stands out from the competition. Pitch a story or lead solely to an editor – or to a journalist on her/his team – and say you will hold it until the next day before pitching elsewhere. This approach also creates an acceptable reason to chase the following morning, bringing your pitch to the top of an inbox.

Editors want an easy 'top line' they can pitch in editorial conferences – something genuinely new, newsworthy and eye-catching/fun. If your pitch hits all these points, an editor is likely to pick it up.

A fully formed pitch with a great top line and no obvious 'holes' is an ideal starting point. Many PR pitches arrive in editors' inboxes without essential information, such as a new venue's opening date, or information on a firm's background or financial backers. Editors will want to verify any information themselves, but offering as much information as possible (succinctly) in a pitch is always a bonus.

What are the business desks looking for?

Business desks look for stories on both listed and private companies. Business reporters want the inside scoop on upcoming start-up raises, company IPOs and deals. The best pitches are those offering exclusive news or insight. Business reporters are also often looking for interesting interview opportunities with CEOs of large or influential companies, and with rising-star entrepreneurs.

What makes a great business story?

What makes a great business story is often the same as a great news story, in the sense that it covers something you would bring up in the pub with friends. The story is easily understood and relevant to consumers' lives. A great business story is also one that makes waves in the business world, and will be picked up by other outlets.

What are some of the key components you need for a good story?

Key components of a good story include: exclusivity; an attention-grabbing top line; new data; a news hook; a 'big name'; great picture.

If someone wanted to get featured in the *Evening Standard*, how would they stand out?

Editors on the *Standard*'s City pages are looking for similar stand-out qualities in interview subjects and stories as journalists on national papers' business desks.

It is always helpful to offer a London or City angle to the *ES*, as it is the London paper and will report in detail on happenings in the capital.

To stand out for the *Standard*, it is also always worth making a press release announcement embargo work for the paper's print deadlines.

The *Standard* goes to print around 11 a.m. each day, so a 6 a.m. or 8 a.m. embargo time can make your pitch stand out, especially for tech firm fundraising stories.

What advice would you give entrepreneurs wanting to get coverage?

The first thing I would suggest is to make sure your message is clear and your pitch is jargon-free. It is very easy when working in any sector to get used to its vocabulary, and forget that jargon can be a turn-off for journalists. A business reporter will understand 90 per cent of the jargon in a pitch, but will then have to translate everything for their readers, creating extra work. It helps entrepreneurs' chances of getting coverage to make explanations about their companies and mission as simple and reader-friendly as possible, while also still containing in-depth information.

I would also suggest that founders and entrepreneurs try to remember a pitch to a business reporter doesn't need to be dry just because there is a financial story to tell. An interesting corporate comms story can also involve elements attractive to consumer business reporters.

Finally, it sounds simple, but if entrepreneurs are looking to get coverage in the business pages, it is always worth working with a PR company with extensive specialist contacts across business desks and at business-focused websites.

For example, if you run a tech start-up, it is worth finding a PR company focused on public relations for tech brands and venture capital firms. This PR firm is more likely to have built up trusting, long-term relationships with tech reporters for outlets such as the *Financial Times*, the *Sunday Times* and the *Standard*.

What doesn't work when it comes to approaching a journalist?
Most journalists are nice people and generally friendly. The one thing I would suggest is to email and/or message rather than phoning journalists' landlines or mobiles directly. Reporters are often on deadlines, in meetings or conducting interviews, and receiving phone calls – especially from unknown numbers – can be distracting.

If you've emailed and then messaged a journalist and they don't reply, it's probably best to assume they are not interested in the pitch, and to get back in touch another time.

Follow Naomi on Twitter
https://twitter.com/nomiackerman

WORKBOOK: USING PRESS RELEASES WITHIN YOUR PR PLAN

Now it's time to get thinking about your story and how you're going to sell it using a press release:

1. Does your business need a press release?

2. What are the most press release-worthy parts of your business plan this year?

3. Who is going to write your release?

4. How will you send out your release?

5. How will you measure the reach of your release?

6. Are there any further assets you need before sending out your release?

CHAPTER TEN

How to Perfect the Email Pitch to Editors

In this chapter, we're going to be looking at arguably the most important part of the PR journey: pitching. We'll be looking at how to write winning email pitches to journalists and editors. I'll be sharing tips on how to write great email pitches, including advice on subject lines, how to succinctly pitch your story idea and how to catch the eye of an editor.

Again, there's a format here that you can adapt and copy – so hopefully I'll be taking some of the guesswork out of the PR pitch. When you're sending a cold email pitch, you really want to stand out and make the email as succinct and effective as possible – editors will get hundreds of PR pitches every day, so the way in which you pitch your story matters.

You'll notice that I've mainly talked about email here – of course, there are other ways to pitch. You may want to go old school and pick up the phone, but I would say to avoid doing this to most journalists; there are a few that might still like the odd phone call, but most journalists I know, especially in the digital space, hate being called and find phone pitches a bit much. Phone calls are for emergencies and crises. It's always a good idea to gauge interest in a story before making a phone call, as cold pitches over the phone rarely get pick-up.

GUIDE: HOW TO WRITE AN EMAIL PITCH

Now, let's dive into how to write a winning email pitch:

FIND THE RIGHT CONTACT

First things first. If you're emailing the wrong person, your pitch isn't going to get seen. So, make sure you've done your homework and found the best point of contact at a publication. As we've looked at in previous chapters, this might be someone more junior at a publication, but someone who has access to story-writing first-hand. There are a few apps you can use on Gmail to see whether your email has been read and delivered to the right place – Boomerang is a particular good one.

WRITE AN ATTENTION-GRABBING SUBJECT LINE

Subject lines are really important. You want to avoid anything general like simply 'PRESS RELEASE' or 'PITCH' (in fact, I would avoid capitals overall as it feels quite shouty). I would always recommend personalising the subject line for each pitch you send out where possible (unless it's a press release, in which it's OK to have a blanket one on email). It's a good idea to personalise subject lines, such as including the name of the publication in the subject line.

'PITCH FOR *GRAZIA*: INTERNATIONAL WOMEN'S DAY SPOKESPERSON'

'PITCH FOR *ES MAGAZINE*: BEST LUXURY HOTELS IN CROATIA'

'PITCH FOR ABOUT TIME: THINGS TO EAT IN LONDON THIS WEEK'

If you've got anything that makes the story special, such as an exclusive, a recent study, stats or talent attached to the story, then mention that in the subject line too. You're more likely to have your email opened if you lead with the best parts of the story in the subject line. I'd also try including a question mark or anything that sparks interest – asking a question is a good way to do this.

MAKE IT PERSONAL – COMPLIMENT

You want to personalise the first line of the email pitch to the editor. I would lead with complimenting something they have recently written, or, otherwise, something relatable that they've recently posted on social media. A little bit of online digging here is useful, just for creating some rapport and warm leads when you send a cold pitch. When in doubt, 'I really love that piece you wrote for X', followed by your pitch, is a good shout.

I know it takes a bit longer to personalise each pitch, but it's definitely worth it in terms of pick-up.

PITCH WITH TWO STORY IDEAS

Now, getting to your main story ideas. I'd always include two or three story pitches in one email – this is because you don't really know what editorial a publication has coming up, and if you just pitch one idea, you might find that they have already run something similar or are planning to. Don't ask if you're OK to send across a pitch, just go ahead and do it. Media is built on cold pitching, it's very standard practice.

Make these story ideas timely and relevant – tie them into national awareness days if you can or use newsjacking to tie them into a current affairs story.

These pitches should be kept to a paragraph each and should share the key information of the story – the who, what, why. Always offer to send across more information, but don't bombard with too much detail in the first instance.

KEEP THEM TO TWO HUNDRED WORDS – YOU CAN USE BULLET POINTS TOO

The key in an email pitch is not to overwrite it. You want to keep each story idea to less than two hundred words and I'd recommend using bullet points to pull out the key facts if you want. If you're suggesting an interview, you can use bullet points to share facts on why the person would be a great candidate for interview. If you're looking for a company to be profiled, mention their revenue numbers, growth or investment – anything that's impressive and adds credibility.

DON'T BE AFRAID OF DOING THE WORK FOR THEM

I would never be afraid of doing the work for a publication. You can break down the information into the format they normally run it in – for example, if you're pitching into a regular listicle, you can use the format of that list and display the information of your pitch in that style. I wouldn't recommend writing up an article in advance of pitching, but do everything but, so the copy is ready to go and the story easy to put together.

IF YOU DON'T KNOW WHERE THE STORY FITS, THEY WON'T EITHER

You need to do your homework to understand where a story fits on a publication. If you don't know where it goes, the recipient won't either. You need to understand what section of a publication a story fits, and if there's a regular column or section it goes into. This is very valuable as you are saving an editor time in placing the story – and a journalist loves a story that's easy to run. You'll only really get a sense of how to do this if you read the publication regularly and have a good feel for the kind of stories their publication runs – how regularly, what time of the week and the kind of content they normally feature.

LINK TO PREVIOUS ARTICLES ON THEIR SITE

An easy thing to do, to give a sense of where your story might sit, is to include links to previous articles of the same kind on their site. For example, on About Time, we have a regular 'About Time You Met' interview slot – if a PR pitches in to this, it's always a nice idea to include a link to a recent interview of the same style as a reminder of what they imagine the story might look like and the kind of coverage they are after.

USE THE PUBLICATION'S HOUSE STYLE AND TONE

It can be a valuable idea to write your pitch in a similar house style and tone as the publication. Again, do an editor's work for them by copying the style of their headlines and the kind of language and tone they use. This just helps the pitch look like something that 'belongs' on the site and gives you an advantage when landing a pitch.

LINK TO YOUR PERSONAL WEBSITE OR ATTACH RELEVANT INFORMATION

At the end of the pitch, always link to a website or social media for further information. Give journalist enough information to get them interested, but not so much that they feel bombarded from the outset. A website link and link to high-res photos, plus a press release attached, should be plenty for an initial email pitch.

FOLLOW UP TWO DAYS LATER

Don't be chasey! It's fine to send a follow-up if they haven't got back to you, but I wouldn't do this for a couple of days. You don't want to be that person who follows up too quickly and ends up annoying the journalist, so unless it's a very time sensitive opportunity, take your time before following up. Again, you can use Boomerang on Gmail to see if your email has been read before chasing.

GOLDEN RULES: HOW TO WRITE AN EMAIL PITCH

There are a few top tips I can share for pitching journalist on email:

DON'T PITCH AFTER 5 P.M. OR ON FRIDAYS

Your email won't get read after 5 p.m. And Fridays are pretty much a no-go in journalism – everyone is looking forward to the weekend too much to focus on commissioning stories and creating new content. Unless it's a weekend magazine, in which case it's sometimes OK to send a pitch on Fridays. I'd always recommend sending pitches out before 10 a.m., as most publications will have a morning meeting to discuss the stories of the day and you want to get in there as early as possible.

DON'T BE TOO FRIENDLY ON EMAIL
Journalism, especially lifestyle journalism, is one of those weird industries where everyone seems to be best mates with everyone. But be careful of being overly familiar on email as this can be a bit of a turn-off – don't call journalists 'love', 'lovely', 'babe' and ask for favours unless you really know them well. Keep it professional unless you have a reason to behave otherwise.

DO YOUR RESEARCH
Always read the publication on the morning of pitching before sending your story, to make sure they haven't already covered it. This is one of the most basic mistakes people make when pitching – it looks quite sloppy and can be easily avoided. If they have already written a story around something you want covered, avoid asking if they can add anything in retrospectively – very rarely is this possible and it looks a little desperate.

OFFER SPEED
If you can deliver something quickly, tell them! Editors love speed and this is a big selling point, if you're able to deliver.

DON'T BE AFRAID TO PITCH AGAIN
Just because one story wasn't right for them or you didn't get a response, don't be afraid to pitch again. Of course, you should avoid pitching multiple times if you're getting no responses at all, but for the most part, editors are always happy to consider new stories and you shouldn't be disheartened if your pitch didn't land at the first few attempts.

QUESTIONS TO ASK YOURSELF BEFORE HITTING 'SEND'
Before you press 'send' on an email pitch, there are a few things to consider to make sure you're hitting the right mark with your story idea.

➡ Why now? What's going on in the news that makes this story timely right now?

➡ Why you? What access do you have? Insights? Experience? Expertise?

➡ What's interesting about this story? Be anything, but don't be boring.

➡ Why would an editor be personally interested in this story? Make sure it's relevant to them and their audience.

If you can't answer any of these questions for your pitch, then perhaps it's time to go back to the drawing board and rework your story for the better.

TOP TIPS:
SECURING PRODUCT PLACEMENT PR

Got a product-based business? Here are some top tips on how you secure coverage for product businesses from Hena Husain, director at *The Content Architects*:

Getting in-product placement is not for the faint-hearted: the competition is high, and there are several factors at play. Here are four tips to help you stand out and, most importantly, get featured!

1. Images should be cropped and ready: From cut-outs to portrait and lifestyle, the very first step is to have your images available in various formats, sizes and backgrounds. Label them neatly – not just for yourself but for media too so they can find them amongst the many others saved in their folders. Ideally your image should be labelled with the product name and company brand. You also want to ensure you have any credit notes on file, along with access to prices and a few sentences on the item itself. By having this at the ready you can react quickly and promptly with the correct

information and imagery (something which only goes down well) when speaking with media.

2. Do your research: Pens and papers, or keypad, at the ready. Look through the target publications and list out the sections that feature product placements and the editors behind them. Note down the level of information shared on each item featured. Pay particular attention to the type of imagery. Do they always use lifestyle images or cut-outs? How frequently does the section run? Pop it into a spreadsheet, use Google sheets, or your trendy go-to software for data. This may take some time, but do it right and it will become the most important tool in your toolbox.

3. React to times of the year: Cultural moments and seasonal hooks are often leveraged by editors – and product placement is no different. By staying on top of key dates you can prep in advance, even offering up ideas to media. You have your retail holidays, such as Mother's Day, Halloween and Easter. When pitching in, think about some of the current trends and what you offer that may tie into them. There are also other key moments such as spring or sports events which can spur on ideas for product listings. Many publications look to run features showcasing products that match up to the chosen hues for that year. But you have to be quick, as soon as the colour is announced – source those images and send it to the right journalists.

4. Photoshoots: When it comes to product placement, there is something pretty special about seeing your product featured on a TV show or an avant-garde themed photoshoot. To have a chance of being featured, media usually want to have a sense of your brand and products already. This means having samples and establishing relationships. By having a good understanding of your brand, even if they are

unfamiliar with that particular product, they have enough of an idea, and reason to get in contact to see if you would be able to send over a sample.

Now let's see some of that advice in action...

MY PR SUCCESS STORY:
LUCY HITCHCOCK, FOUNDER OF PARTNER IN WINE

Name: Lucy Hitchcock
Age: 30
Job title: Founder of Partner in Wine

How successful have your PR campaigns been?

PR campaigns have driven tens of thousands of pounds' worth of sales for my ecommerce business Partner in Wine. The secret to the success of these I would say has been relevant placements, and profiling me as the founder as opposed to the products themselves.

What do you think has helped you get press?

I have gained a huge amount of organic press simply from the story of my business. Granted, not everyone has a heart-warming story such as mine, but everyone certainly has a relatable story to tell. If you can write your brand's story in a captivating way then you can sell anything.

What's the best thing you did to support your business and its press appeal?

A mixture of branding and storytelling. First of all, if your branding isn't appealing to a social media-obsessed world, then it's unlikely that the press will see this appeal either. Things to get clear on: Making sure your social media matches your website, sticking to your brand guidelines, and making sure you have photography and videography that matches your brand feel. You need to try and make your brand as appealing as possible with content that matches your story!

How do you use Instagram to build your press appeal?
I use Instagram not only to connect with my customers, but I've found it's a great way to connect with journalists too! Many journalists have followed my story, and enjoy following it to this day. I regularly put out engaging, entertaining and informative content which people tend to stick around for. It's not all about posting your products or services, it's about curating an engaged community who will buy from you time and time again. Once you start making more sales from social media, I suppose that's also an angle to write about – lots of articles that have been published about my business regularly include sales stats from viral videos.

What makes your business press-worthy, do you think?
Partner in Wine is a very new business, and the reason it's press-worthy is both the success story of how I started it in lockdown along with a viral video that changed Partner in Wine into a six-figure business overnight. People also absolutely love connecting with the founder of a business these days, and I am constantly talking about the business and updating people online, which all have a direct impact on the type of press requests I receive. I rarely receive product feature requests, but I do receive requests to interview me as the founder.

What has attracted journalists the most to the story of your business?
I started an insulated wine bottle business in lockdown due to a problem I faced when the pubs were closed. I wanted to be able to have a socially distanced drink with friends outside, but there was no way to keep my wine cool – and I had the idea for a chic wine cooler and Partner in Wine was born. During a time that has been really quite tough on most people around the world,

it's always nice to hear a success story that has come out of something so awful.

What advice can you give start-ups about launching and getting press for their business?
Start telling your story on social media, and once you feel confident enough telling that story start reaching out to the press. Make a list of your ideal publications (whether you're working with a PR freelancer, agency or doing it yourself) so that you know what you're aiming for.

What would you do differently if you could go back in time?
Nothing. I've been lucky enough to ride an amazing wave of viral videos and press articles every single month! Any mistakes I've made along the way, I've taken as a lesson, and I think that's a hugely important part of running a business.

WORKBOOK: PERFECTING THE EMAIL PITCH

Grab a notebook and brainstorm what you've learnt in this chapter:

1. Who are the right journalists for your stories right now?

2. How confident are you with pitching writing?

3. What's happening in the world right now that ties into your story ideas?

4. How much time in your schedule are you going to dedicate to pitching? When will you do it?

5. How can you stay on track with this? What will hold you accountable?

CHAPTER ELEVEN

Continuing Your PR Momentum

In this final chapter, we'll be looking at all the ways you can continue to build PR momentum within your business and daily actions that will take you closer to your goals. In this book, we've explored lots of different routes to garnering press coverage – from producing your own podcast to putting on events, working with influencers and pitching media – but it's worth remembering that these actions in isolation won't have a lasting impact, and it's important to keep working on your PR plan as your business develops.

You may want to experiment with different activations as your business grows in reach and revenue and introduce new elements to your PR plan. There may also be a point at which you'll want to work with an external PR agency to take your reach even further, and, if so, I've provided some expert insights on how to successfully hire and work in partnership with an agency.

Let's start by diving into some good habits that can build your PR momentum and keep your PR appeal at the forefront of your business:

DAILY HABITS

BUILD RELATIONSHIPS
There are opportunities to build relationships with journalists every day, but you must stay alert to see them. Start by engaging in conversations that are happening around you online – whether that's a journalist sharing their feature or an editor asking a question about a travel destination. Look for ways to build a 'warm' lead before approaching with a story – being of service and helpful

to others is a great way to build relationships without the 'ick'.

The best investment of an entrepreneur's time is cultivating relationships with journalists, editors and freelance writers. Start with researching their individual interests and areas of expertise before any outreach; communicate by email and stay in touch via social media between pitches, and be generous, even when you don't need anything from them.

Once you've built relationships on social media, you can take things a step further and try to meet face to face or pitch them story ideas, but start by putting yourself in their world and listening to the conversations happening around you.

SET A FOCUS FOR THE WEEK AHEAD

Take Sunday night to think about what you want to achieve in the week ahead. With PR pitching, you really need to block out some time to get it done, so find an hour every day that you can devote solely to your outreach. I find the best time to pitch is first thing in the morning before journalists' inboxes are bombarded with pitches and press release, so if you can dedicate an hour every morning to sending out three to five pitches, that will benefit your PR plan loads. PR pitching really is a numbers game, and the more pitches you send out, the more likely you are to receive coverage.

When planning before the week starts, consider these things:

⇨ Check in with your goals and priorities – what's the most important thing in your PR plan right now?

⇨ Check your schedule – if you're not able to dedicate time in the morning, use the evenings to get prepared and have emails scheduled to go out at 9 a.m.

⇨ Have clear objectives for the week – where do you want to be by Friday? What would a successful week look like?

⇨ Map out key tasks in your PR plan for each day – what daily action would take you closer to your goals?

⇨ Write out a detailed plan for Monday morning, so you're not feeling overwhelmed when the week begins.

⇨   Get an accountability partner – who can you share your PR plan with? Who will hold you accountable and check that you're meeting your objectives for the week?

NEWSJACKING

Newsjacking is the process of adding your thoughts and opinions into breaking news stories – and it can be a great way to keep your brand relevant and add value to news stories.

Get into the habit of reading the news every day and finding ways that you can contribute to the conversation – whether this is on social media, through online content or a press release. Start your day by reading the day's headlines and think of ways that create relevancy with your business and what's going on in the world. Short daily news podcasts, such as 'Today in Focus' by the *Guardian* and *The Times* news briefing, are also very handy if you're short on time and want to know the key details of what's happening in the world.

TAKE NOTE

It's very easy once you're caught up in the day-to-day of your business to lose sight of the bigger picture and you may miss great potential PR stories if you're not paying attention to what's happening in your business and how it relates to the wider world. So, get into the habit of daily note-taking of anything interesting that happens in your business, which might make a good PR story, or any ideas you have for pitches.

I keep a list of notes in my phone, which I add to whenever inspiration strikes – this might be an idea for a story, a challenge I've recently overcome or something I've seen on social media which has sparked a conversation or opinion in my head.

STAY RELEVANT

Relevancy is so important with business, especially relating to your PR plan. You want to stay relevant by reading and reacting to the news, but also by producing relevant content that resonates with your target audience.

Research awareness days and include them in your content-planning calendar to ensure your social media is as impactful as possible. Being relevant also means being seen – make sure you're posting every day and showing up for your audience; this helps maintain momentum and will have a knock-on effect with your PR plan too. Being 'out of sight, out of mind' is true for social media too. Being relevant also means being responsive and flexible; when a breaking news story happens, you want to react quickly and be able to provide quick commentary or insights that will support a journalist in their story.

ADD VALUE

Whatever actions you take in your business, you always want to be thinking about adding value. You should add value through your social media channels with lively and informative content (this will help set you up as a thought-leader too) and through the content you post online. If you focus on the value you're bringing to your audience, rather than the number of followers, you'll find you naturally attract more PR attention as your business will create a stronger sense of authority and trust within its own space. Keep up with what's happening in your sector and add value by reacting to this online.

ENCOURAGE LINKEDIN POSTING

I've mentioned LinkedIn for your personal brand previously, but the value of LinkedIn is collective too, and you should be encouraging your employees (especially anyone at senior level) to be posting on LinkedIn too. This will help build the credibility of your business and more of a following around it – which will only benefit you long-term. You want to be showing the behind-the-scenes of your business, its working and ethos through these platforms, so encourage your employees to share their positive insights and experiences through working with you.

STAY CONSISTENT

Showing up online matters; it demonstrates to your audience that you're present, reactive, and current. But posting once or twice won't have lasting effects – what matters is continuing to show up, staying consistent to your personal social media and marketing plan. The same applies for PR; you want to be consistent in sending out pitches, responding to news stories and coming up with content ideas. It's not something that can be done in a fit, in a moment of inspiration, but rather something that works best when performed weekly with a clear goal in mind. Inconsistent actions get inconsistent results – staying consistent with PR means putting a schedule and plan in place that you can commit to, for at least six months, to really start seeing results.

PROMOTE YOUR COVERAGE

It's easy to forget to celebrate the wins when you're caught up in the doing of your business but sharing any coverage you do get is very helpful for building PR momentum. Remember to share any press coverage across your platforms and make them easy to find on your website – you might want to do an IG or LinkedIn post sharing the content or do some talking-to-camera stories about the coverage. Create a highlights reel on Instagram called 'Press' where stories that feature PR wins are saved and pin some coverage to your 'Featured' section on LinkedIn to make it easy to find. Journalists will look for credibility with their case studies and showing the coverage you've already received is a great way to show value and demonstrate your press appeal.

LONGER TERM

Want some longer-term investments for your PR plan? Here are some ideas of things you can do to keep building PR momentum:

HIRE A PR AGENCY

There may be a point where you want to hire an external agency to help you with your PR plan. There's no perfect time to hire an agency, but only consider it when you've really given your own PR plan a go – you may find you don't need one and you're perfectly capable of doing your own outreach, and it's a great skill to develop.

That said, you may find that you're too stretched on time to really commit to pitching and need some additional support with your PR plan – or you might be operating in an industry that has very specific contacts that an agency can reach more easily. If you're ready to delegate this part of your business plan to an agency, don't rush into the relationship and get very clear about what you want from it.

INSIGHTS: CHOOSING A PR AGENCY

Emilie Lavinia is the founder of TENTH MUSE GROUP and co-founder CEO EKHO wellbeing. Here she shares her thoughts on how to hire the right agency for your business:

Running a business means overseeing myriad moving parts, each with their own costs and KPIs, and this can be stressful and challenging, especially for small businesses. This is why outsourcing and delegation are so essential. But here's the thing, as a business owner, you have to manage your expectations and recognise that whomever you hire, they're not you. They'll support you but they don't have your vision or your passion for your business. It's up to you to communicate that vision and passion to the best of your ability so that they do get it. This will create a value add for you and for your supporting network of businesses and contractors.

Next, the fit has to be right. The amount of times I've seen a small FMCG business match up with a huge corporate firm that specialises in celebrity or a huge event company take on an inexperienced solo contractor is too many times to mention. It's vital to hire a PR who understands your business model, has the right contacts and experience and can offer strategies that suit your products and services.

If you're hiring a multi-service agency, always ask about additional services, bespoke packages and the level of support you can expect. And once you're confident you have the right fit, allow your PR to impress you. PR and Marketing require skill, strategy, a wealth of contacts and knowledge and the ability to work reactively to a rapid news cycle. If you're confident to outsource, place your trust in your PR and allow them to support you. Backseat driving will slow them down and dilute their work.

Lastly, it can require a real leap of faith to trust someone else with the telling and retelling of your brand story, especially if it's a personal one. You're allowed to shop around. PRs will pitch you to win your business and obviously, given that they pitch for a living, their pitches will be crafted to impress. Take time with your decision, ask questions and speak with a few companies to ensure the fit, the cost, their expertise and their approach are right for you.

https://www.emilielavinia.com/about

GOLDEN RULES: HOW TO HIRE A PR AGENCY

Considering hiring an agency, but don't know what to look for? Julia Linehan founded The Digital Voice in 2012 and specialises in digital communications, PR, event content creation and thought-leadership content. Here's her golden rules on hiring an agency:

1. Chemistry is key

A response to a request for proposal (RFP) is fine but chemistry is a far better gauge on whether you are a good fit. A good PR agency will become an extension of your team so you need to get on well and hold similar values.

2. Match your style

Some clients are cautious, corporate, strategic and have

multiple layers of sign off. They need to find a more established, corporate agency who has a similar style. Start-ups who are snappier, fast paced, willing to take risks and be bold might suit an independent PR agency more.

3. You know when you know

Don't look at a long-winded review process. Write a succinct document with what you want to work on with an agency. Keep questions simple and to the point. Focus on asking the questions that align with finding out if their strengths sync with what's required from the partnership.

Proposals back should be kept brief and one interview with the stakeholders on both sides should be enough. If you're not convinced after the first meeting, they're probably not the one for you.

4. Smoke and mirrors

Get references from current clients to ensure that what an agency promises they'll deliver, they actually will. A good agency will be transparent. A good MD of an agency will be hands on. A good reputation is absolutely essential.

INVEST IN VIDEO

Video is fast becoming the most popular content medium. Video can really help when integrated into your PR campaign – you will be able to show and tell your story in the quickest way, with visual appeal. News outlets want this, as does the consumer.

Across the social media and digital industries, it's becoming apparent that the value of having visual media is essential to build digital audiences. The way things are going, video content is becoming more popular every day. To use video effectively as part of your social and PR strategy, you must get clear on what platform you want your video content to be shared on and how you aim to generate interest around your video. Putting an executive on camera to talk about your brand or story will always be more interesting that just a written medium – and it will help show the person behind the story and inspire others.

Video might be a useful addition to a press release, for example, which brings your story to life, or you may want to use video assets alongside your story pitch that a publication could include in their article. Or you may want to use video content on TikTok to demonstrate your product business in a fun, engaging way. Plan ahead – allocate resources and budget for this, as generating good-quality video can take some time – but it can be very valuable for your overall outreach strategy.

INVEST IN CONTENT

If you want to build credibility within your business, you need to invest in content – this might mean hiring an expert content creator, a freelance writer or copywriter. Website content really matters for how you are packaging and describing your business – this is where storytelling will help advance your brand value. Investing in content is a cost-effective approach and all your copy will help you gain media opportunities – blog posts, social media and website copy all play a valuable role in your PR plan.

The more you invest in content, the more chance you'll have of earning effective backlinks, which is crucial for a digital-first PR strategy and directing users to your website. A successful publicity campaign is about having stand-out copy from content creators that really understand your business and can reflect it in the best possible light.

START AN AMBASSADOR PROGRAMME

An ambassador programme, which is a more comprehensive version of influencer marketing, is a great way to support your PR plan. With ambassadors, you'll have more people naturally promoting and endorsing your business and extending your reach on social media. Ambassadors will promote your brand in exchange for commission, free products, or a fee, and this will help with word-of-mouth for your business. You're more likely to receive new business if you have people who are promoting your business in a positive light and helping to spread the word.

SPONSOR EVENTS

Another way to amplify your brand and increase visibility is through partnerships. This may involve sponsoring events, such as large sporting events, conferences within your industry or an event in your local area. Again, evaluate the cost versus opportunity here and whether it will benefit your brand enough to justify the expense involved. You want to sponsor an event that carries a strong positive message and offers a good impact-focused outcome for your business. There are lots of benefits to partnering on a big event or expo, however, as they will often have their own PR and marketing campaign that you can be included in, and you'll have the additional resource of their own PR team supporting your business.

MEDIA TRAINING

Finally, you may want to invest in media training for yourself or your staff to take your PR plan one step further. Media training can help you develop yourself as an authority within your business – it will help you come across as confident, comfortable and relaxed in media interviews. Media training can also be useful for crisis management, if your company needs a spokesperson to handle a situation and be a confident leader in moments of crisis. Media training will give you strategies for answering questions in an effective way and how to present yourself in the media as a positive, confident public figure.

WORKBOOK: CONTINUING YOUR PR MOMENTUM

In this final chapter, we've looked at some additional daily habits that can continue PR momentum for your business. Take a moment to consider these questions and the plan you'll put in place for your business:

1. What daily habits are you going to commit to your business?

2. How will you stay consistent and committed to these habits?

3. What return would you like to see on your daily actions?

4. Are there any additional things you'd like to invest in for your PR journey?

5. Would your business benefit from an ambassador programme or event sponsorship? How will you get started with those?

Conclusion

Throughout this book, we've gone on a journey together finding how to create world-class publicity for your business. I hope you've learnt first-hand that you don't need to have a huge budget or team to get started with PR, and everyone can benefit from having a well-considered PR strategy. And that really is easier than you might think; once you've discovered a great story, there are some quite simple steps you can take to get the attention of the press.

As we've discovered in the book, publicity looks very different in the digital age – it's not just how others talk about your business, but the actions you can take to boost your own publicity and self-promote through social media, podcasts and events. Everything in the publicity world starts with confidence; talking confidently about your business, having the confidence to put yourself out there and the belief that your story is one that needs to be heard.

Believe that you're able to achieve this on your own. All the great stories lie within you, and once you learn to package them with style and ease, you'll be flying.

I wish you all the luck in the world for your publicity journey and I can't wait to see what you achieve with the guidance within this book. I hope to see your name in lights very soon indeed.

Acknowledgements

I'd like to thank my publishing team for their support on this book; Tom Asker at Little, Brown for being a most calming and reassuring presence, and Florence Rees at AM Heath for being simply the best agent in town. Thank you to Geraldine Collard, who believed in me for writing my first book and has been a mentor in publishing ever since.

Thank you to my flatmate Aimee for not getting annoyed as I re-boiled the kettle a million times while writing this book. And to my dog Alfie, who kept me company during many late-night editing sessions – you'll never read this, because you're a dog, but I hope you know how loved you are.

To my best friends Gemma, Claude, Adam, I am so grateful for your words of encouragement and endless support, and to Chez and Carla for just being the best pals a girl could ask for. To Bex, thank you for being my forever work wife – I'd be lost without your guidance. And, finally, thank you to my family, Suzi, Oliver, Elizabeth, Howard and James, for always supporting my writing career – Mum, you're my creative inspiration and I owe you so much.

Index